S0-CBL-711

When Mabel Laid the Table

When Mabel Laid the Table

The Folklore of Eating and Drinking in Australia

Warren Fahey

**STATE LIBRARY OF
NEW SOUTH WALES PRESS**

Published in 1992 by State Library of New South Wales Press
Macquarie Street, Sydney 2000, Australia

Copyright © Warren Fahey 1992

Edited by Jacqueline Kent
Designed by Deborah Brash/Brash Design P/L
Picture research by Joanna Collard and Kate Irvine
Typeset by Post Typesetters
Printed in Sydney by Southwood Press

National Library of Australia
Cataloguing-in-publication data:

Fahey, Warren
When Mabel laid the table: the folklore of eating
and drinking in Australia.

ISBN 0 7305 8900 5.
ISBN 0 7305 8901 3 (pbk.).

1. Food — Folklore. 2. Folklore — Australia. 3. Food habits —
Australia. 4. Drinking customs — Australia. I. Title

398.355

Title page: Picnic at the Blue Mountains, NSW, 1923

Contents

Federation Day picnic, White Cliffs, NSW in 1901.

Introduction

THIS is really a social history of eating and drinking in Australia. It shows that we in fact have a unique tradition of wining and dining, Australian style, that started expressing itself from the very early colonial days and has never stopped.

In many ways, our history is a rough-and-tumble sort of affair, as pioneering histories tend to be: anyone with even a slight knowledge of it knows that 'Mabel' did much more than simply lay the table. The pioneering women had to invent and improvise when it came down to producing a fixed number of meals for a family, with very limited resources. And we have gone on from there.

I have taken various aspects of our culinary history and placed them in historical context. Subjects covered include food in colonial times, the traditions of the bush cooks, cookery during the lean times of the 1890s and 1930s Depressions, what Australian kids eat, how we celebrate festivals and social occasions such as weddings and twenty-first birthday parties, Australian etiquette, what and how we drink, and the changing role of restaurants.

I should point out that I do not regard myself as a gastronomical expert, considering myself to be more of a bush cook and culinary observer who is interested in all things Australian. I have long been fascinated by the folklore we all create and preserve in the normal course of our lives. History books give us statistics, but I am more interested in what could be called the 'emotional' history of Australia, the history of its people, for this has always given the real answers.

A quick glance through the book will show some very familiar recipes. I have gone for the obvious, especially those endangered culinary species such as sago plum pudding, pikelets and rabbit pie. Being particularly indebted to all those people who have contributed recipes, I have decided to print every item as given, which means that there is some inconsistency in temperature and measurement. This swings from imperial to metric. I consider this fair revenge for all those times I have had to scratch my noggin over post-metric recipe books! Some of the native animal recipes may be considered slightly shocking, but they too are part of our culinary heritage. Like the recipes, they have come from ordinary Australians, and present an entertaining guide to our attitudes about eating and drinking.

Students of the Emily McPherson School of Domestic Economy, Melbourne, *c* 1924.

Acknowledgements

This book could not have been written without the pioneering work of all those 'Mabels', women and men, who created an Australian cuisine from sheer necessity and not much else — or without the latter-day 'foodies' who wrote about, talked about and enthused about what 'Mabel' has laid on Australia's table for more than two hundred years.

Thanks are due to my many friends and correspondents who enthusiastically passed on family recipes and kitchen wisdom and to Annette Zubani who advised me, 'When you're asked for a recipe always leave out one ingredient so that nobody else can cook it as good as you.' To my 'food mafia mates' for their continuing campaign to wave the flag of Australian cuisine — Joan Campbell, Cherry Ripe, Leo Schofield, Michael Dowe, Sheridan Rogers, Carol Baker, Greg Doyle and Gay Bilson. Long may they wave their spatulas! To the late Joe Watson who cooked great damper, corned beef and plum duff. To publisher Rod Mead for serving up this book and my editor Jacqueline Kent for making it more palatable. Thanks also to the State Librarian, and Mitchell Library staff of the State Library of New South Wales.

But I wish particularly to thank my mother, Deborah Phillips Fahey, who was a deft hand in the kitchen and who taught me the intricate skills associated with pot-scouring and washing up. I also want to thank Mark Cavanagh, Astro, and all my friends who have both rejoiced and suffered at my table.

An early start to the day for Kathleen Peel, Kyabram, Victoria, *c* 1912.

1

How Mabel Laid the Table

THE image of Mabel and Mum preparing Sunday lunch for Dad and Dave is a colourful one that owes a lot more to our pioneer film industry than to reality. Sure, times were tough in the backblocks, and sometimes there wasn't a lot of tucker. But the imagination and initiative of Australia's pioneer women produced more creative menus than do many of today's Mums and Mabels.

Much of the folklore associated with our eating and drinking originated in colonial Australia, when a bunch of early settlers found themselves isolated in the bush. We adopted, or adapted, many of the old customs and traditions of the home country and added others that 'just seemed right' for outback life. We Australianised the recipes of old Britain and Ireland, substituting available ingredients and even changing names to sound more Antipodean. Many a side of kangaroo appeared on the dining table under the guise of prime roast beef, and the occasional wombat reappeared as a smoked English ham. We also experimented to create local dishes that owed more to Mother Nature than to the great cookbooks of Europe.

Inventive bush cookery very much depended on where people lived. River folk ate codfish and mullet, while isolated station owners were forced to eat native fruits, wild pig and kangaroo. The coastal people had the full fruits of the sea and those 'in transit' fed on salted meats and other dried foods. After the goldrush days of the 1850s and 1860s, transport improved and fresh supplies arrived regularly, especially via the efficient riverboat system, unless of course (as was usually the case) the river was in drought or flood.

The first settlers looked on the Aboriginal diet as scant and uninteresting. However, this attitude merely showed the general ignorance and misunderstanding of Europeans. In reality, the Aboriginal communities enjoyed a wide range of foods including poultry, wild rice, grains, seafoods and nuts. Much later the more adventurous pioneers learned somehow to make Aboriginal dishes, and 'bush tucker' became an important part of every travelling bushman's survival knowledge. I have spoken to many old bush hands who have deep respect for the Aborigines, and nearly all of them dipped their hats to the fact that 'there's no way you would starve in the bush if you were with an Aboriginal stockman'. Native potatoes or yams are well known, but many other vegetables and fruits were to be found, as well as ways of getting water and hunting wildlife.

Pigweed was the most widely used of the native greens. The small leaves and stems are quite succulent when boiled, but could also be eaten raw. Various other greens were harvested, including so-called New Zealand spinach, groundsel and wild cabbage. The native fruits included sandalwood, desert lime and emu apple and gave much-needed moisture to many a thirsty traveller. Sadly, we now realise that the colonial government's attitude to transplanting European agricultural methods resulted in the eventual devastation of many prime Aboriginal food source areas, particularly the river areas.

Our colonial cities were essentially mirrors of London — or at least that's what the locals wished to believe. By the turn of the century Sydney, for example, was a hubbub of commerce, with a very lively port area, the beginnings of a city and a population hungry for comfort. The first twenty years of settlement had seen the colony run as a large military barracks with the soldiers running as wild as the convicts and an economy that somehow or other ran on the currency of rum. At one stage the fledgling metropolis boasted some two hundred licensed alehouses and a total population of only about twenty thousand. These taverns were far worse in many ways than anything to be found in the London dock area and the licensees more unscrupulous than the typical London rogues; many were ticket-of-leave convicts who thought nothing of dispensing a 'dram' made from a hideous mixture of cheap rum, water, tobacco, burnt sugar and anything else that could add to its punch. This lethal drink did nothing to improve the reputation of the town or the health of its inhabitants.

As New South Wales was a penal settlement, Sydney was designed as a large military base; not until the 1830s did the administrators begin to consider town planning and urban welfare. In 1833 the first Sydney market development was officially opened, with regulations aimed at warding off

A rare drawing of street life in Sydney, 1849. The Skinner Family Hotel, situated on the corner of George and Hunter streets, was typical of the bed and board hotels that serviced the colony. This one was also licensed to sell 'fermented and spirituous liquor' including 'london porter'. Today a skyscraper sits on the site. The streets were obviously steeper than they are now.

disease, particularly bubonic plague. Designed by Ambrose Hallen, the markets were an impressive addition to the city and they soon became a gathering point for almost the entire population.

The early city markets must have presented an extraordinary sight. The population had been used to the markets of England and Ireland, but here the produce was very much 'mutton dressed up as lamb' with dubious health control and even more dubious produce. Licences were not required and accordingly all manner of goods and services were hawked and squawked.

By the 1850s Sydney and Melbourne had expanded to such a size that simple coaching inns gave way to larger hotels and boarding houses. In Sydney the Royal Hotel even boasted a successful dining room with regular theatrical productions.

A colourful and seemingly accurate picture of rum-sodden Sydney is provided by the journal of Nathaniel Pidgeon, a self-appointed evangelist who conducted Bible-thumping prayer meetings in gold-fever Sydney. 'This has been a remarkable day,' Mr Pidgeon wrote on 1 May 1853, 'three persons I had been attending died today, two women and a man, both the women killed themselves with intoxicating drink!' He then went on to point to the fact that the previous week 90,000 gallons of beer, 70,000 bottles of beer, 34,000 gallons of brandy, 2600 dozen bottles of brandy, 31,000 gallons of gin and 48,000 gallons of rum had been landed in Sydney. 'By a rough calculation,' he wrote, 'it would appear that one gallon of beer, a pint and a half of brandy, a pint and a quarter of gin, and a quart of rum had arrived for every man, woman and child in the colony.' He went on to warn Sydneysiders of the arrival of the 'poison' and the fact that the Licensing Board would be responsible for more deaths than the Russian War.

It is also a fact that isolation caused drunkenness and the fledgling colony was considered to be at the very end of the world. Most colonial inhabitants regarded alcohol as a 'cure' for such ruination and the official reports indicate that 'the streets were awash with drunken men, women and children', whilst on 15 June 1837 the *Sydney Herald* complained that 'a person could not turn a corner without running into a drunken beast'.

A sly grog tent on the Ballarat goldfields. (The same sign can still be found in most corner pubs.)

It is easy to understand how Australia was considered a strange land that offered unbelievable opportunity and equally unbelievable deprivation. The rich compensated by importing the very finest cutlery, dining room furniture and even grand pianos; they hired servants, many of whom were ticket-of-leave convicts, and they played at being in England by demanding menus that ran the full gamut of a London eating house, complete with imported wines and ales. By contrast, the poor comforted themselves with food from the coach and ale houses and the street vendors of pies and saveloys.

Our cities must have been colourful and extremely noisy. Street cries were delivered in a sing-song style that would identify the particular seller.

The street vendors also had to compete with 'official' criers and noisemakers. The city watchman had the duty of being the 'public clock'. On the hour, every hour, he would ring his bell and shout out the time with an added 'all's well'. He wore a special watchman's uniform and carried a long staff that one can only assume was used when all was *not* well. The 'bellman' was another early identity; his job was to ring the bell and shout out the governmental orders of the day.

But as a collector of folklore, I am more interested in the cries of the common folk. The loudest and more frequent calls were given in a Cockney/ early 'Strine' accent, along the lines of these attributed to a Mr 'Socks' Cameron: 'gen-u-ine latest fashion — 4d a pair or a bargain lot for a deener! Step up and I'll sock you 4d a time!' Or this one from 'Lord Much' McCoy: ''Ere y'r ladies and gentlemen, step this way. New model ladies' shoes for three and six a pair. Kickers fit for a countess!'

Sydney's street-selling backyards included a pipe clay seller, a buttermilk man who walked the streets crying, 'Buttermilk for a fair lady's complexion' and the watercress man with a cry of 'Water Cree..sesses', complete with a drawn out 's' to make any snake proud.

Fish alive-oh! Fish alive. All alive here and kickin'. Come and try and buy and try — anything under a bushel for 6d — Alive-o, Alive-o, Fish alive!

Mullet-o. Mullet-o. Fresh whitin'! Feel 'em and try 'em, taste 'em an' buy 'em.

Cherry ripe, cherry ripe. Fresh as daisies and sweet as sugar. Cherries at 2d a pound.

Oysters 6d a plate — don't be late — oysters!

Ripe strawberries, turn and try the strawberries. Roll up and buy the strawberries fit for pies, jams and all sorts! Fine ripe strawberries.

Half a sheep for half a crown!

Quoted in the *Australian Journal* 16 September 1868

• The Flying Pieman •
Tune: 'The Flying Dutchman'

*'Twas the close of a heavy drinking bout
    on port and sherry cape
From public, half seas over, we had just
    made our escape
Our infant in its cradle was peacefully
    asleep
And merrily we rolled along the street of
    Church Hill steep.*

*At length Bill Tompkins gave a shout of
    terror and of fear
As though he had just gazed upon some
    stern policeman near
We looked all down the pavement, cried
    Tompkins, 'Well I'm blowed
See where the Flying Pieman comes
    bounding over the road!'*

*He come, the Flying Pieman comes, and
    terrible his pace
He scuds along the flinty path as though
    he ran a race*

*The cards and placards in his hat all
    pasted on awry
Are circulated quickly as the Pieman
    dashes by*

*He scudded on too speedily to mark his
    rapid flight
In fear and consternation then we
    staggered off, half-tight
Quoth Tompkins, 'When we travel home
    I fear there'll be a breeze
Our better halves will put an end to
    these delightful sprees!'*

*Then mark the Flying Pieman, for
    comical his doom
He scuds about from morn till night,
    queer costume doth assume
Around the town he beats about, for
    every night and day
And boys, admiring shout, 'There goes
    the Pieman .. hip hooray!'*

From the *Colonial Society* magazine 1869, under the section 'Songs For All Hands'

'Do you sell pies?' asked the gentleman as he strolled into the George Street pastrycook's shop. 'Oh yes, sir, all kinds of pies, sir,' replied the girl behind the counter. 'Well, give me a magpie!' 'We do not keep them, sir but I should say that you wouldn't have much difficulty finding one further out — they say birds of a feather flock together.'

From the *Australian Journal*, 1867

The Flying Pieman was undoubtedly Sydney's best known hawker with a reputation for extraordinary feats of endurance and eccentricity. Once he walked, with his tray of pies, from Sydney's Circular Quay to Parramatta and beat the Sydney-to-Parramatta ferry. The Flying Pieman wore an old frock coat of different coloured patches and his hat being covered with tickets and placards and his legs and feet in hessian bags.

Reminiscences of John McIntosh, 1839, quoted in *Old Times* magazine, 1903

One of the most energetic areas of street vending seems to have been the hawker of snack foods, particularly the hot saveloy man. Many ditties are dedicated to him; saveloy men apparently had a street language of their own with such terms as 'throat cutting', where the saveloy was slit down the middle and sprinkled with vinegar. Some of the sellers had carts, others simply strapped a small portable saveloy cooker to their chests. It was common to give your stove a name like The Spirit of England or John Bull's Best. The saveloy sellers had a common cry of, 'All Hot!' to which they sometimes added, 'What d'yer choke yer mother with? Hot saveloys!'

One of my favourite saveloy songs is actually an early music-hall parody of 'If Those Lips Could Only Speak' and has a story that includes a talking, winking saveloy.

He stood there and gazed at that sausage,
It winked and then gave him a kiss
And said, 'It'll cost yer a tanner
If you want your jaws around this'.
Then his lips he gently moistened,
He felt pains in his inside,
With his eyes fixed upon that sausage
He murmured before he died:

If those tongues could only speak,
If those pies could only see,
If that large piece of roll and sausage
Were mine in reality,
Could I grab it in my hand
And bury it once and for all,
Though it's only a beautiful sausage
In a beautiful coffee stall.

Early music hall song, Australian Folklore Unit collection

The street crier also acted as a travelling newsman. The Hon. John McIntosh MLC was reported in *Old Times* magazine of 1903 as remembering 'Saville, the Sydney town crier and bellman who announced such things as auctions and lost children. "Oyez! Oyez! Hear you peoples that this day a child has been lost in the scrub wearing a blue dress and hat with pink ribbons. Anyone giving information of its whereabouts to the distressed parents will be handsomely rewarded. God save the Queen!" '

As the country opened up, the hawker played an important role in outback Australia. In many cases, he was the only supplier of such household essentials as buttons, sewing needles, pots and pans and books. Many hawkers were Indian or Afghan traders who had originally travelled to

A fine colonial building, this one, and the enterprising proprietors even offer a wash basin for those grimy customers ready for a pie and coffee dinner. One can only guess at the contents of those early 'mystery bag' pies.

Australia to work on the railways. Some even travelled the roads complete with turban, camel and family. The Afghan hawkers introduced real spices to our early cooking; they sold an impressive range of spices and curry powders as they moved around the bush. The cry 'The Afghan's coming down the track' meant a spending spree that would often leave Mum beaming and Dad scratching his skull. The descendants of these hawkers can still be found in Australia, especially operating country haberdashery stores.

George Loyau, also known as George Chanson, in his *Sydney Songster* published between 1865 and 1869, included a minstrel-type song about a hawker called the Ham Fat Man.

> *The Ham Fat Man, he fell deep in love,*
> *All with Sara Ann, to be his turtle dove;*
> *She dwelt in Sydney market, number 13 was her stand,*
> *And she sold polony sausage to the Ham Fat Man.*
>
> *Ham fat, soap fat, candle fat or lard,*
> *Ham fat, cat fat, or any other man;*
> *Jump into the kitchen as quick as you can,*
> *With my roochee, coochee, coochie, the Ham Fat Man.*

———— • ————

A Sydney merchant made it the boast that he had never given away a shilling in his life. One day a poor Irishman stepped inside his establishment and looking very upset, said: 'May it pleze your honour, I've lost a pig, the only little piggy I ever had. My mistress has sent me to you to see if you would be kind enough to give us another — just a small one would do... We haven't money to buy one ourselves.' Whereupon Paddy set up such a wailing and a howling that the merchant took a pound note out of his pocket and gave it to him — just to stop the commotion. The next day the merchant happened to see Paddy in the street and chanced to ask him whether he had bought a pig with the money or foolishly spent it in the tavern. 'Of course I bought a pig,' Paddy declared indignantly. 'Well, let's hope that you take better care of this one,' said the merchant. 'We don't want any more lost pigs running around the town. By the way, how was it that you happened to lose the last one?' 'Well, now,' said Paddy, 'we ate him!'

Australian Journal, 1866

———— • ————

The standard bush home basically consisted of four slab walls and a fireplace with a small cabinet for storage, a table, chairs and a bed. Pioneers did with what they had and that was very little. Faced with the option of buying kitchen luxuries or a shovel, axe or bucket, there was little choice — practicality ruled every time. Once the home had been constructed, the pioneer family set about making furniture, children's toys and kitchen tools out of appropriate timber and junk — and clever they were, too. Very few recipe books were taken into the bush. Very few were available, and most of the population were poor readers; besides most of the ingredients were unobtainable. Mrs Beeton's now-famous *Book of Household Management* was not published until 1861 and, although it was the first truly popular cookbook, it came too late for a generation of pioneering women who were faced with the terrible problem of 'What will I serve the family on Sunday?'. The answer was to be a combination of traditional family recipes, half-remembered, half-invented recipes and some gleaned from neighbours. What the pioneers did was write their own recipe books and it was a matter

I shall rehearse
In rhyming verse
Our life
In this Antipodes
The day we're fed on pork
*   sans bread*
Or biscuit stale with
*   Adam's ale*
Thus first we starve
But soon we carve
Roast cockatoo
Starved kangaroo
Fine parrots blue
A rare emu
But this does not content ye
Although of such rich plenty
Old English taste
Bids mutton haste
And prays for beef
As some relief
From kickshaws so outrageous
John Bull must eat
His honest meat or soon
He gets rampageous

From the book 'The First Australian Colonists' by Margaret Stephenson, wife of the captain of the *Buffalo*, 1838

Bushman's Chutney

Take a quarter of a tin of dark plum jam and two tablespoons of Worcestershire sauce. Mix together and serve!

Joe Watson, 1973

This early settlers' 'home sweet home' is typical, the major furniture being those very large sea chests that would have transported all sorts of goods and chattels to the colony. Note the foxtails pinned to the wall.

of household pride to collect such recipes, index them and file them in manuscript books. True to tradition, these recipes travelled down the years in the same way that traditional songs were orally transmitted.

As farms improved, the pioneers built themselves cookout huts or lean-tos that later became known as 'the kitchen' and often became structural parts of the house. Other small huts were built as needed — a slaughterhouse, meat smoking room, bread baking house, storeroom etc. As the stations got larger, better kitchen facilities were installed, including bread tables, an array of cooking pots and implements, a meat safe, water filters and kitchen safes to protect food from the inevitable flies and ants. Insects were always the scourge of the Australian bush and the pioneers invented all manner of things to protect their foodstuffs. The four legs of the kitchen safe would stand in old jam tins full of water, or the meat safe would be suspended high from a nearby tree.

On the grand properties it was fairly common to hold a celebratory dinner whenever a major farm building had been completed. These feasts, in the tradition of the British 'harvest home', were a way of thanking the workers, family and neighbours. The group would sit down to a 'farmer's dinner' of kangaroo soup, huge meat pies, boiled legs of mutton, peas and suet puddings with beer and porter to wash it down.

Not all squatters were so generous. Late in the nineteenth century, the bush rang with tales of James Tyson better known as 'Hungry' Tyson. Tyson (1823–1889) was an Australian-born pastoralist and millionaire landowner, who reputedly deserved his reputation as the meanest man in Australia. One tale tells of Tyson employing a young ward of the state to work in his household. When a girl arrived it was discovered that she was suffering from sandy blight, a common disease causing diminished eyesight. Even though the girl could hardly see, she was immediately put to work. It was Tyson's habit to carve the meat for the evening meal so as to limit the amount of rations provided.

One evening, as he passed the plate to the young girl he quizzed. 'And how are your eyes, young lady?'

She replied, 'Poorly, sir, I can hardly see the meat on my plate.'

Next evening, as he passed the thin slice of meat, he questioned, 'And how are your eyes this evening?'

'I think they're getting better, Mr Tyson,' replied the girl, 'I can now see the plate through the meat!'

Another Hungry Tyson yarn concerns Tyson telling his stockhand he had arranged to feed them both while they were out fencing. At lunchtime Tyson produced two eggs which he boiled and proceeded to eat. As he scoffed the eggs down his worker protested, 'But Mr Tyson, you said you'd bring my lunch!'

'And I certainly have,' snarled the squatter, as he pointed to the water that had boiled the eggs, 'Egg soup!'

The pioneers devised all sorts of ways to keep flies from spoiling food. They cleaned their windows with a cloth soaked in kerosene or paraffin oil, they moistened an old rag with oil of lavender and left it near the open windows, cloves were hung from the candle-holders and pots of fennel were placed in strategic places. If all that failed, they made a fly paper by cutting strong brown paper into strips and soaking them in alum, allowed them to dry then coated them with a mixture of boiled linseed oil, resin and honey.

The rush to the diggings in the early 1850s created large tent cities where food was generally in short supply, controlled by goldfields merchants who set up 'tent stores'. Native foods were far cheaper than potatoes and flour, but the goldfields store owner usually made more money than the miner. These stores offered a wide range of merchandise, including baking powder, imported tea, chicory, preserves and condiments as well as clothing, household furnishings and books. Still, the Australian goldfields saw the extremes of starvation and excess; jubilant miners on the Victorian goldfields would

Feed the man meat! Captain Frazer and his family dining at home in Ballina, NSW, 1896. The meal seems to consist mainly of meat and bread, with not a vegetable or salad in coo-ee, let alone a glass of wine or beer. Note the bush lemons hanging from the lamp and the quinces on the sideboard.

Apparently business didn't give a lot to smile about. This goldfields store at Gulgong, NSW, would have offered a limited but essential range of stock, including fresh fruit and vegetables, fuel, matches, cooking pans, gold-digging equipment and some grocery lines. They were all very expensive.

drink champagne while lighting their fat cigars with a five-pound note while at the same time, miners were starving to death on the way to the remote Palmer River in Queensland. A common story in gold-crazed Melbourne concerned miners striking it rich and hitting the finest restaurants, where they would order two slices of bread and then proceed to put a ten-pound note between them and eat it.

As gold strikes were announced, the rush would move from site to site, state to state, leaving a trail of tracks that became roads, shanties that became hotels and miners who became farmers. It was the discovery of gold that really opened up Australia, increasing the demand for an organised communication and transport system. By the 1880s there was a workable network of roadways and riverways that transported the wool, beef and wheat down to the cities and returned laden with supplies for the station owners.

Flour was the most important ingredient in the bush pantry and Australians made a culinary artform out of the wheat 'dust'. Bread, damper, Johnny cakes, puftaloons, doughboys, pikelets, scones and many other foods owed their existence to flour, water, salt and not much else.

• Johnny Cakes •

You need flour, water, salt and bit of baking powder. It's pointless giving quantities as it all depends on the state of your ration bags. Cut a sheet of bark from an available tree and use the clean side as a mixing dish. Build a good fire and let it settle as hot coals. If your best water is full of mosquitoes and flies then skim with a spoon, stick or rim of your hat to remove foreign bodies. If your water is muddy and you have plenty of time you can clean it with muddy wood ashes. Anyway, mix the ingredients into a stiff dough and make into cake sizes — say eight to ten inches diameter by an inch thick. Cook both sides and eat.

We were in a pub one night and a stranger who was looking for cooking work boasted that he could make at least fifteen kinds of pastry out of a pannikin of flour. An old geezer in the corner of the bar eyed the stranger up and down and reckoned he would put him in his place. 'Well,' he groaned, 'you reckon that fifteen is a good number, but when I was shearing down the Bogan we had a cook called Feathers who was a master of the flour art. He would serve up twenty-five different types of pastry and we had to make sure all the windows were shut otherwise they would float out the windows — they were that light!'

Cooking Bread in a Wet Camp

(Where wood is scarce and sufficient embers for a camp oven fire are difficult to obtain.)
Boil a kerosene tin three-quarters filled with clean water. Grease inside your billy and place your bread dough inside allowing for about a third of the billy for the bread to rise. Put a bit of clean rag on top of the dough and jam the lid on tight and plunge the billy into the boiling water. It will cook nicely.

Joe Watson, Caringbah, 1974

FINEST AUSTRALIAN ROLLER FLOUR

While travelling once I came upon a man in a tent who was very anxious for me to stay to dinner. Said he would have a damper cooked in a jiffy; pulled off his shirt, poured some flour on it, and started to mix. Have myself used a corner of a tent, and even a saddle-cloth, when nothing better was to be had; but that dirty shirt made me suddenly remember that I was in a great hurry.

The Bulletin 17 September 1898

• Mermaid Brawn •

Ingredients: One dugong. As they weigh up to 200 lbs, this is a recipe for a large dinner party. Boil a large chunk of dugong along with some buffalo shin or ox tongue and add some salt, pepper, cloves and any other suitable spice. Boil and remove fat. When it is well cooked chop it all up and press into a suitable dish for brawn, draining off the excess liquid to allow for setting. Serve sliced with salad or damper.

———— • ————

We were camped on a lonely part of the Darling River, and as our meat supply had been exhausted, we decided to try cooking some galahs that we managed to trap. After boiling all the afternoon they were still as tough as old boot-leather so we boiled them another hour or so, and drank the soup, throwing the bodies to the dog. Later I asked a bushman the correct way to cook a galah, as I had been told it was a common item on the bush menu. This bushman told me that the only successful way is to get a farrier's rasp and file the galah to a powder. Mix with water and make a soup.

From the World News

———— • ————

In truth, galahs and other wildlife were frequently served in early Australia. On the next page is a genuine recipe.

Cornstalk Sandwiches

You'll need four beaten eggs, three-quarter pound of sugar and one and a half cups of self-raising flour. Beat eggs and sugar together for about twenty minutes then add flour and bake for ten minutes.

Bungaree Porkato Sandwich

Take one large cooked potato and put it between two cooked pig's ears and eat.

Roast Bandicoot

Bleed the coot immediately after the kill then scald and pluck the hair off. Clean and leave soaking in a strong salt concentrate for half a day. Wipe and dry the coot clean then stuff with breadcrumbs and onions and cover with a few strips of bacon (to improve the flavour) and put the whole lot in a large brown paper bag and bake in the oven. It is important not to have the oven too hot or the skin will crack.

Galah

One of the most beautiful birds in the bush is the pink and grey parrot known as the galah. They are tough old birds. Take six freshly killed galahs, pluck and clean them in preparation for boiling. Place in a billy with some onions and available seasoning. Place a clean axe head in with the birds and boil until the axe head is soft — the galah will now be ready to serve.

Popular bush joke

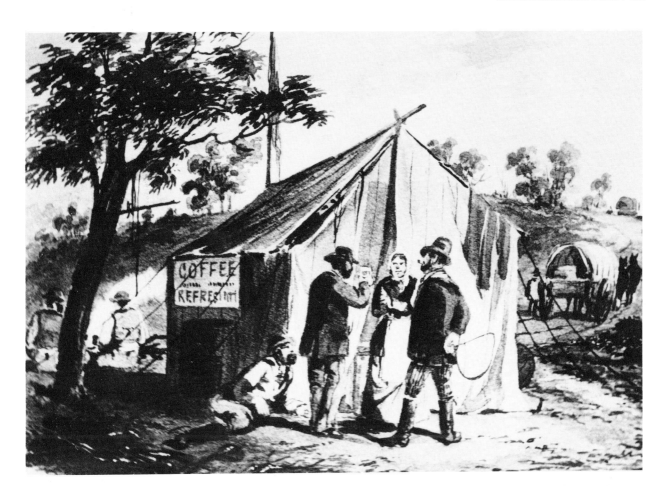

A coffee, refreshments (and sly grog) tent on the Victorian goldfields.

First catch your galah, but be careful how you pluck them for this is what makes them tough. Add half a teaspoon of salt and one of sugar for every galah you have in the pan. Roll them in flour and fry them in melted butter or fat until they are golden brown. Then add available vegetables and the juice from the frying pan and a good dollop of Worcestershire sauce and simmer for an hour and a half.

The kangaroo has been the staple diet of the Aborigines for many centuries, and it is interesting to see recent moves to introduce it to fashionable restaurants in our tourist-laden cities. The kangaroo does make for clean meat and all parts are good to eat except the feet, which are pure bone and muscle.

• Kangaroo Tail Soup •

In order to make this satisfactorily the meat must have been killed for some time or it will possess no distinguishing flavour; yet care must be taken not to use any portion of the meat tainted. If in the bush where kangaroo is plentiful, the stock may be made from the same instead of beef or veal. Cut up the meat into proper sized pieces and place into a saucepan with about 3 or 4 lbs of the meat from the leg or any other part, a slice of ham or lean bacon, two blades of mace, two onions, celery, marjoram and seasoning. Add 4 quarts of light stock; place on fire and cook gently until the tail is thoroughly done. Drain liquid and thicken it with brown roux to the proper consistence; cook gently for half an hour, take off all the scum or fat, put in a large glass of madeira or similar wine. A large tablespoon of red currant jelly and the juice of a lemon and pieces of the tail. Boil and serve.

Australian Journal, 1879

• Tailing a Kangaroo •

*Bill Swiggen and myself were bush'd up
    in the mallee scrub
For two long days and two long nights
    we had not tasted grub
And on the third, my blessed word,
    affairs looked rather blue
When Bill descried with joyful pride, an
    old man kangaroo.*

*This old man quite majestically sat
    upright on his tail
He looked at us contemptuously, nor did
    he shake nor quail
He seemed to say, 'To come this way,
    what business friend had you?'
'By Jove!' cried Bill, 'I'd like to kill that
    old man kangaroo!'*

*Without another word he rushed with
    waddy in his hand
To where the old man kangaroo
    undauntedly did stand
He aimed a blow, this hairy foe upon
    poor William flew
And grabbed my mate, as sure as fate,
    this old man kangaroo.*

*He clasped him tightly in his arms and
    Bill began to roar
A struggle so terrific I had ne'er beheld
    before
'Oh Tom, why blow my eyes, he'll break
    my back in two
Come hither quick and fetch a stick —
    oh, cuss the kangaroo!*

*At my approach the kangaroo made
    ready for a bolt
But still he clung to William tight, he
    would not lose his hold
But Bill, you see, was twelve stone three,
    flesh bones and muscle too
That's overweight, the truth I state, for
    any kangaroo.*

*Then stealing up behind the brute, my
    bag I opened wide
And pulling it down over his ears, I
    then securely tied
It round his neck, this seemed to check
    his progress so I drew
My dover out and with a shout, I tail'd
    that old man kangaroo.*

*A kangaroo without a tail can't run we
    all well know
So finding his appendage gone he let
    poor Willie go
He gave a shout, a gory tail I tell you
    but it's true
Then with a jump he sunk, a lump of
    lifeless kangaroo.*

*My mate was slightly bruised about but
    scarcely was he free'd
When turning round to me he says; 'By
    George, we'll have a feed.'
Then Billy put on the billy-pot and
    cooked a splendid stew
And the sweetest meal I ever ate was
    that old man kangaroo.*

Published in the Australian Journal (1871) and attributed to Tom Tallfern. This song
has been collected on three previous occasions as 'The Old Man Kangaroo'; however, this is the original
version and obviously not a music hall composition as previously thought.

• Bushies' Kangaroo Tail Soup •

Remove the hair and clean the tail then cut into strips to fit your cooking pan. Bake for about two hours with a little salt and fat. Peel off the skin and cut into pieces then roll each piece in flour. Put the meat into your pot with water to cover, adding salt, pepper and available herbs. Some chopped bacon is also good for the soup. Halfway through the cooking add some chopped carrots, potatoes and onions. Simmer for one and a half hours.

Mrs Petti Watson

———— • ————

Usually mild, inoffensive animals, kangaroos are sometimes stirred up to wrath when brought to bay by dogs; and there are two instances on record in the Bothwell district, of 'boomers' (Forester Kangaroos) having seized men in their arms, and carried them for some distance, and then flung them violently down. I have seen the haunches of a 'boomer' which weighed ninety-six pounds, and stood seven feet high.

Memoirs of Hull in Australia, undated

Kangaroo Mince Pies

Boil 1¼ lb of diced roo steak until tender then mince meat. Allow meat to cool then blend in a mixture of ½ lb suet, 1 lb each of currants, raisins, three cooking apples finely chopped, 1½ cups of white and brown sugar, 1 teaspoon of cinnamon, the juice and grated rind of two lemons and two oranges. Simmer for about half an hour then pack into sterilized pressured jars. Store in a cool place until Xmas.

Australian Journal 1870

Baked Roo Tail

The Aborigines have a very simple recipe that involves placing the tail directly on the ashes. The hide is left on and the meat sizzles and cooks to perfection.

• Kangaroo Steamer •

This is a braise where the kangaroo meat is steamed. Cut the meat into pieces of about a quarter of an inch square, and put in a pan with a well covered lid, with a spoonful of milk, a chopped onion and some salt and pepper to taste. When it has been on the fire for a short time add about a tenth in quantity of salt pork, or bacon cut to the same size as the kangaroo meat. Serve hot with spiced jelly.

Of all the dishes brought to the table, nothing equals that of the steamer. It is made by mincing the flesh of the kangaroo, and with it some pork or bacon. The animal has not any fat, or scarcely any, in its best season. When the meat is chopped up, it is thrown into a saucepan, and covered over with the lid, and left to stew or steam gently by the fireside. It only requires pepper and salt to render it delicious. No one could tell what a steamer is unless it has been tasted; it indeed affords an excellent repast; and it is surprising that the kangaroo steamer, preserved in tins, has not been exported to England.

Melville's Australia, undated

———— • ————

Bill Harney, that great bushman of yesteryear, had a favourite saying about native food: 'If it moves, catch it — it might be good tucker'. In his cookbook he mentions many bush recipes including crocodile and turtle egg dishes, possum pumpkin pie, baked bandicoot, roasted goanna and witchetty grubs — all cooked in bush style. Bill Harney also passes on a great piece of Aboriginal wisdom: 'If you want food to go further, eat less.'

Selling Port Macquarie lobsters at Kempsey NSW in 1907. The same would cost a pretty penny today.

• Fritters for Tea •

*In the bush of Australia, as you all
are aware,
There is plenty of hardship and very
rough fare;
With sugar, flour and fat I am sure
you'll agree
A man can turn out some nice fritters
for tea.*

Chorus
*Oh, don't I like fritters, lots of nice
fritters,
Plenty of fritters and sugar and tea.*

*The English like pudding, the Scots
like burgoo,
The Paddy delights in a good Irish stew;
But George, Pat and Sandy will all say
with me,
'There are many things worse than nice
fritters for tea.'*

*One day, to my grief, I got lost in
the bush,
When attempting for home by a new
way to push;
I thought as the sun went down I
could see,*

*'Here's a poor chance for some fritters
for tea.'*

*Two days and three nights I wandered
forlorn,
My legs were quite tired, and my clothes
were all torn,
My trousers were all battered right up
to the knee
But the thing that grieved me most was
— no fritters for tea.*

*One Sunday it was when I went on
the lurch,
I prayed for a cook-shop much more
than a church,
I groaned as I lay at the root of a tree,
'Oh, I wish in my heart I had some
fritters for tea!'*

*When safe and sound I got back to
my home,
I took jolly good care for some time not
to roam;
That night you may think I pitched in
with great glee
To a wonderful feed of nice fritters
for tea.*

From the Hurd Collection, Oxley Library, Brisbane

• A Rhyming Recipe for Bread Sauce •

*A penny loaf procure, discard the crust
But of the crumbs retain as much as just
Will fill a teacup and then on it pour
As much new milk as it will soak or more
To this within a pan you must surely place
Twelve corns of pepper or a little mace
One onion add, about the middle sized*

*To impart the flavour so highly prized
Upon the fire now set it, there to boil
Whilst gently stirring 'till it is quite stiff
Add to it then two tablespoons of cream
(Or melted butter if this better seem)
It is now ready but I pray observe
Take out the spice and onion ere you serve.*

Australian Journal, 1878

Native animals were also common fare in the cities. In the 1870s Melbourne and Sydney street hawkers regularly offered wild duck at 7s 6d, swans for 2s 6d each, rabbits at 6d a pair, bush turkeys for 3s each, as well as wild pig, koala and kangaroo meat. Early Australians became the greatest meat eaters in the world, and it is interesting to note that butchers were one of the first trades to become organised on a wholesale and retail level.

All Australian cities were becoming aware of the need to organise the commercial side of food supply to meet the demands of the growing population. In Sydney, the convict-era markets, situated towards the southern end of George Street, remained in use right up to 1891 when the Sydney Council began pulling down the structure to make way for the copper-domed Queen Victoria building. But traders and customers preferred the

*Antipodean Culinary Couplets
(a Rhyming Epicure)*

*Veal cutlets dipped in egg and
breadcrumbs,
Fry 'till you see a brownish
red come
In dressing salad mind the law
With two hard yolks use one
that's raw
Roast veal with rich stock
gravy serve
And pickled mushroom to
observe
Roast pork sans apple sauce
past doubt
Is Hamlet with the Prince of
Wales left out,
Your mutton chops with paper
cover
And make them amber brown
all over,
Brush lightly your beef steak —
to fry it
Argues contempt of Christian
diet.*

*To roast spring chicken is to
spoil 'em
Just split 'em down the back
and boil 'em
It gives true epicures the
vapours
To see boiled mutton minus
capers
Boiled turkey gourmands know,
of course,
Is exquisite with celery sauce
The cook deserves a hearty
cuffing
Who serves roast fowl with
tasteless stuffing
Roasted in haste a haunch
of mutton
Might make ascetics play the
glutton —
But one might rhyme for weeks
this way
And still have lots of things
to say
And so I'll close, for reader
mine,
This is about the hour I dine!*

Australian Journal, 1868

Imagine the look of horror on the face of the local council health inspector. This turn-of-the-century butchery would have offered basic cuts of chops, steaks, roasts, offal and snags. Shoppers would have needed to be early to beat the blowflies.

Black Swan Casserole

Cut ½-inch steaks from the breast and back legs of a swan. Coat well with flour, seasoned with pepper and salt. Layer bottom of casserole with swan meat and cover with onion rings. Add another layer of meat and onions then sprinkle with about 1½ tablespoons of flour. Push five or six bay leaves down between the meat. Mix together and then pour the following mix over the meat: 2 cups of water, ½ cup of tomato purée and two tablespoons of red wine or sherry. Cover and bake slowly for two to three hours.

Australian Journal, 1872

older market sites at the Haymarket and the would-be market became offices. Melbourne's Eastern Markets flourished in a grand Victorian structure covering two acres that became a major social focal point. Street hawkers also roamed the cities selling pigs' trotters, oysters, baked meats and pies, and nearly every busy street had an open-air coffee stall emitting a strong smell of burnt sugar and chicory.

Restaurants of every size and style were also being built to cater for the hungry hordes, especially the newly rich citizens. In the 1850s, a chain of fourpenny and sixpenny restaurants was established in Melbourne by David T. Way, an English emigrant. By all accounts, one was likely to find 'more flies in the dishes than refined prejudices might fancy'. For the more affluent or particular Melburnians, there were Langlois Luncheon Rooms and Scots Pie Shop in the Royal Arcade, where diners could eat three courses for a shilling, with a glass of colonial wine for 3d. There were also 'fancy' restaurants serving quality designed foods aimed at the gourmands.

In Sydney, restaurants began to appear on every possible street corner, the most popular offering 'all you can eat for one shilling'. King Street was well known for its oyster bars, where patrons could dine on lavishly prepared seafoods and oysters 'straight from the shell'. There were also many fine restaurants, including Adam's Cafe in George Street, Adolphe's Parisian Diner on Hunter Street, Compagnoni's in Pitt Street and the dining rooms of the grand hotels. The Metropolitan Hotel in Pitt Street advertised 'a spacious garden at the rear, with tropical trees, etc. Arbours and seats, a delightful retreat for the hottest day of summer'. Another famous eatery was the Cafe Restaurant Francais, in George Street, where the attendants spoke all European languages and the landlord, Mr John Poehlman, provided an impressive French cuisine and imported wine cellar. When the cafe was enlarged in 1854, the *Illustrated Sydney News* commented on, 'This attractive temple dedicated to the genius of French cookery', and added, 'our

English readers will doubtless imagine, when they hear of a restaurant being established in Sydney, that the most *recherché* plates will consist of kangaroo steaks or parrot pie... until the opening of this very excellent restaurant, we are quite of the opinion that Sydney was immersed in the thickest darkness in culinary matters... those who have a taste for something better than too-recently-killed mutton or sodden beef, may here gratify their palates.'

Oyster bars were also extremely popular in all Australian cities, reflecting the growing interest in coastal city life. In Paddington, an inner-city suburb of Sydney, there were no fewer than eight oyster bars operating up till the beginning of this century. Not all grand parlours, these bars offered a tempting range of seafood and ale in a no-nonsense setting.

As respectable eating places opened in the cities, they set a standard which had a positive effect on the more affluent households where 'keeping a good table' was a sign of social success. Meat was still considered the major food; it was common for meat to be eaten by all social classes at all three meals. Our pioneers also ate far too much of everything, which explains the corpulent figures that scatter our history books. A typical lunch would include soup, a meat joint and sweets with cheese and salad, whilst the evening meal would consist of soup, beef or mutton, roast or boiled, potatoes and vegetables, bread and butter pudding and cheese and fruit to follow. It is amusing to consider that, although food seemed bountiful, there was often an acute shortage of glasses, plates and cutlery.

It was a matter of great pride that our colonial cattle provided superior meat, much sought after by other countries. Our restaurants served up 'whopping great slices of beef' accompanied by equally large servings of potatoes, pumpkin and peas and then flooded with a heavy gravy. This song, from colonial South Australia and dated to 1860, tells of how Australian beef was preserved and despatched to England where it was sold cheaper than the local meat.

Creamery butter, fresh eggs, prime bacon, Arnott's biscuits and fresh dates. All at Pardey's in Albury, NSW, 1907.

● The Boiled Beef of Australia ●

(Tune: The Roast Beef of Old England)

Hurrah for the meat now our own's got
*   too dear*
They're bringing preserved from Australia
*   to here*
The workman can add to his bread and
*   his beer*
The tender boiled beef of Australia,
Oh, the Australian boiled beef!

The butchers will shake in their shoes I'll
*   be bound*
With their chops and their steaks at a
*   shilling a pound*
A joint for poor folks that are touch'd
*   and unsound*
For now we've the beef of Australia
The tender boiled beef of Australia
Oh, the Australian boiled beef!

When juicy boiled beef is the artisan's fare
He'll find it at once inexpensive and good
At fivepence a pound, fat and bones
*   will exclude,*
For now we've the beef of Australia
The tender boiled beef of Australia
Oh, the Australian boiled beef!

So let us from all the stale rubbish refrain
Some butchers oft sell for exorbitant gain
And stick to the beef that's brought over
*   the main*
For now we've the beef of Australia
The tender roast beef of Australia,
Oh the Australian boiled beef!

Oh the boiled beef of Australia . . .

2

Who Called the Cook a Bastard?

THERE was a popular Australian folk saying that ran: 'Who called the cook a bastard?' to which the inevitable reply came, 'Who called the bastard a cook?' This disparaging attitude to mass-produced Australian food was applied to mess-halls of the armed forces, boarding house dining rooms and the dining huts of the outback stations. Whilst much of this mass-produced food could, at best, be described as 'edible', the songs, yarns, poems, and stories written to immortalise the cook have greatly contributed to our national perception of Australian cuisine and to the philosophy that hard living meant hard tucker.

Life in the Australian bush was hard and very much a male-dominated society. Men came to the bush for several reasons and one feels that food was fairly low on the priority list, as long as there was a goodly supply of mutton, damper and tea. Itinerant workers — shearers, drovers, bullockies and fruit pickers — moved from camp to camp and state to state seeking work. A bad cook was expected; a good one was indeed a blessing. Cooks also moved from camp to camp. Many spent equal time in the city and the bush, and more than one moved up bush to 'dry out' from city alcohol. Traditionally, a cook (or 'Cookie' as he was affectionately known) was a man who was either too old or too useless (or both) to work. As a rule, cooks travelled out to the stations with the shearers and if more than one cook happened to be offering his services the men would vote. Where there was no cook on the camp the men were known to draw straws to see who would take on the terrifying task of cooking with bad rations for men who had bad tempers. Many the cook became handy with both the saucepan and the knuckle.

He was lazy
He was cheeky
He was dirty
He was sly
But he had a single virtue
And its name was rabbit pie

Files of the Australian Folklore Unit

Here I stopped
Here I shook
I ate some damper
From Si Dunnes' Cook.

Files of the Australian Folklore Unit

I remember a cookie we had up on a Queensland station. He was a big ugly brute named Fighting Foley. We all thought that his nickname was in honour of the great boxer Larry Foley, but we were wrong. He was a terrible cook and every day we'd leave the hut whingeing loudly so he could hear us. Well one night he came in with his usual pot of stew and plonked it down saying, 'This here is stew and any man who disagrees can meet me outside!' One of the shearers, a big burly fellow, thought he'd try it on and went outside. Ten minutes later he comes in with blood on his face and sat down quietly muttering, 'It's bloody stew all right!'

Rad Dawson, Forrester's Beach, NSW, 1973

This old bush cook (c. 1926) looks like an Afghan, so maybe that's a cous-cous hiding behind the sugar-bag. The sturdy forked fireplace has major boilers and the team looks ready and willing to hoe in.

The Australian sense of humour comes from our pioneers, so we tend to have more in common with the American tradition than that of Mother England. We have seen the hard times and laughed because there was nothing else to do. Faced with an endless diet of mutton, bread and tea, bushmen responded with jokes, yarns and verse.

You may talk of your dishes of Paris renown,
Or for plenty through London may range,
If variety's pleasing, oh, leave either town,
And come to the bush for a change.

On Monday we've mutton, with damper and tea;
On Tuesday, tea, damper and mutton
Such dishes I'm certain all men must agree
Are fit for peer, peasant or glutton.

On Wednesday we've damper, with mutton and tea;
On Thursday tea, mutton and damper,
On Friday we've mutton, tea, damper, while we

With our flocks over hill and dale scamper.

Our Saturday feast may seem rather strange,
'Tis of damper with tea and fine mutton;
Now surely I've shown you that plenty of change
In the bush, is the friendly board put on.

But no, rest assured that another fine treat
Is ready for all men on one day,
For every bushman is sure that he'll meet
With the whole of the dishes on Sunday!

By F. Lancelott, quoted in *Australia As It Is: Its Settlements, Farms and Goldfields.*
Lancelott was a surveyor in the colonies.

One of the main problems facing the outback cook was the continuing lack of supplies; there is obviously a limit to the number of dishes that can be made out of salted beef, dried vegetables, salt, flour and water. Occasionally one of the sheep would disappear and for several days mutton would appear in various guises, but then it was back to the inevitable salted beef and damper.

Another major problem was that the shearers and drovers worked very hard and developed ferocious appetites. 'They would eat four lamb chops, four eggs and damper for breakfast and by morning smoko they would be demanding another feed!' according to Col Bowen of Forbes, NSW, in 1974.

The folk character Crooked Mick is well known, and his huge appetite has been well documented. Mick was reputedly born way outback at a time when the Jenolan Caves were wombat holes and Uluru was just a pebble. He grew and grew until his parents sent for a Wauchope woodchopper who ring-barked his ankles. Eventually young Mick became a shearer and, being a hard worker, he had an immense appetite. At breakfast he would devour at least four sheep — six if they were weaners — two dozen eggs, thirty-three slices of bacon, fourteen large dampers, a gallon and a half of tea and, when they were available, three watermelons. He always said, 'A shearer needs fuel.'

Some bushmen weren't shy about eating horses; in the European tradition horsemeat appeared on the menu in a few camps. The following nursery rhyme parodies appeared in the 1860s.

Sing a song of horse-flesh
Or hippo-pha-gy
Three screws served up
In boil, roast and fry
When the screws were eaten
The guests began to sing
Isn't this a dainty dish to set
*   before the King.*

Ride a stock horse
To the kitchen, of course,
To see him stewed down to
**   puree perforce**
Use his liver for patties
For jelly his toes
And eat him up clean
From his tail to his nose.

Hey diddle diddle
Horse loin in the middle
Horse soup in everyone's spoon
The little dogs fear
Their supply may run short
And the knackers may shut up
**   shop soon.**

Hickory dickory dock
Horse makes capital stock
A horse-steak fill on
And you'll eat 'till it's gone
Hickory dickory dock

Adelaide *Advertiser*, 1860

'We used to call our Cookie Jesus because he could turn bread into stone!' was one quip about a particularly awful cook.

———— • ————

I'll tell you about the largest damper in the world. It must have been at least twelve feet in diameter and was cooked on a large bullock wheel . . . Paddy Doolin and I were travelling along this road after a couple of successful magic lantern shows. On the horizon I could see a cloud of dust and a group of men riding on horses. They were armed with poles and were obviously intent on bashing our heads in — they thought we were the escort for the strike breakers coming up from Victoria, the home of scabs . . . there had been a savage strike at the time and the shearers were all camped by this river, waiting for the scabs to pass through. Luckily one of the shearers recognised my mate Doolin and they invited us to join them at the camp. Well, there it was being made, this huge damper that would feed the four hundred striking shearers. They had it with cockies' joy — it tasted good because it stuck to your ribs!

Joe Watson, Caringbah, NSW, 1973

Damper

Take about 3 lb of flour and put it in a dish, adding a good pinch of salt and a combination of 2 parts cream of tartar to 1 part bicarbonate of soda. Pour some water into the dish and mix it into a light dough. Sprinkle some flour over the bottom of the camp oven to prevent the damper from sticking, then put in the dough and put the lid on top. The best way to cook the damper is in a hole in the ground and then cover it with hot ashes. It must be completely covered or it will burn. It will take about half an hour to cook and the best way to test it is to scrape off the ashes, lift the lid and tap the dish with a stick. If it gives a hollow sound it's ready to eat. The best way to eat damper is with cocky's joy, which is better known as golden syrup.

Joe Watson, 1974

The shearer's cook, resplendent in white apron, poses with the shearers and presumably, the boss. Photographed at Walgett, NSW, in 1926.

Brownies simply use a damper mix with the addition of sugar, currants or raisins. The standing bush joke is that when you haven't any dried fruits use dead flies — nobody will know the difference, besides, a little protein never hurt anyone!

The outback station cook was paid by the men and it was customary to 'pay the cook his fee' at the end of the season. This might have been a way of 'controlling' the cook and encouraging the best results and, if he had been extra good, it was also customary to 'sling a tip'.

• The Station Cook •

Oh you should taste his doughboys, his
  plumduffs and his pies
I swear by Big Maloney they'd open a
  shearer's eyes
He gets up early in the morning, makes
  us plenty of stewed tea
And don't forget when shearing's done,
  to sling the cook his fee.

But oh dear, I feel so queer, I don't
  know what to do
The thought of leaving Fowler's Bay,
  it breaks my heart in two
But if ever I get that slushy, I'll make
  him rue the day,
That he spoiled my constitution, while
  shearing at Fowler's Bay.

Old bush song

In a similar vein is the old bush song known as 'Gilliat Mug the Cook', the last verse of which advises the shearers to run for Epsom salts or any other stomach cure.

Gilliat Mug the Cook

Bring along your pills and
  potions, Epsom salts and
  castor oil,
Any new ideas or notions that
  will make your stomach boil;
If you're inclined to doubt it,
  well come and take a look,
All the hungry swagmen shout
  it, 'Gilliat Mug's the bloody
  cook!'

Collection of the Folklore Council of Australia, 1974

A shearer was out west and looking for work when he came across a huge mob that seemed to run for miles. It took him an hour and a half to get to the head of them and there was this bloke sitting on a horse. 'Good day,' the shearer said. 'Are you with these sheep?'

'Well, yes and no,' came the reply, 'I'm with the dogs and I've got fifty-three of the devils.' The shearer was eager for work and pressed the cove for information on the station. 'Well, they belong to an outfit called the Burraweena Pastoral Company and as far as I know they are always shearing to keep up with the mob.' 'Strike a light!' said the shearer, 'it must be a bloody big shed'. 'Oh, it's a big shed all right. I don't know much about it except that they have forty cooks just to cook for the cooks. Yes, it was a pretty big show.'

Dick Roughley, Bathurst, NSW, 1973

The shearer had earned a spree in town and headed down to Adelaide where he decided to hit the high spots. His first stop was in a swish restaurant where he ordered tea and cake. The waitress delivered the tea and a lovely fresh carraway seed cake when the shearer commented: 'I see you've had a mice plague down here, too!'

Up in Queensland the sugar cane industry attracted many a bush cook who thought to escape from the grumbling shearers. Cane cutting, like shearing, was backbreaking work and the cutters worked up big appetites, and grumbled frequently. Later cane cutting attracted Italian and Maltese workers who tended to bring their own cooks.

• The Cane-Cutter's Lament •

How we suffered grief and pain,
Out on the Isis cutting cane,
We sweated blood, we were black as sin,
For the ganger he put the spurs right in.

The first six months, so help me Mike,
We lived on cheese and half-boiled rice,
Doughy bread and cat-meat stew
And corned beef that the flies had blew.

The Chinese cook with his cross-eyed look
Filled our guts with his cornbeef hashes,
Damned our souls with his half-baked rolls

That'd poison snakes with their greasy
*   ashes.*

The cane was bad, the cutters were mad,
And the cook had shit on the liver,
And never again will we cut cane
On the banks of the Isis River.

And we're leaving this lousy place,
We'll cut no more for this lousy bugger;
He can stand in the mud that's as red
*   as blood*
And cut his own flaming sugar!

Australian Folksongs of the Land and Its People, Folklore Council of Australia, 1974

Cooks in the bush have to practise their art under considerable difficulty. The general provision for cooking consists of a large open fireplace with perhaps a single chambered iron oven set into one corner. A fire of big logs is needed to constantly boil a fountain of hot water, over which all culinary work is done. When these conveniences are absent, what is known as a 'camp oven' is used. This is a cast-iron, flat-bottomed vessel, from eighteen to twenty inches in diameter and nine inches deep with perpendicular walls, two loops for a movable handle on opposite sides and three legs about three inches high. It has a lid to fit on somewhat loosely with a loop on the top about for lifting a hook. The camp oven is used for baking bread and cakes, for roasting joints, for frying, for boiling or any other of the ordinary purposes of a cooking pot. It is equally useful in a big fireplace or at a campfire and it is always carried by teamsters and professional bush cooks.

Recollections of Mr J. Creed (1842-1914), Mitchell Library, Sydney

How to Cook a Roast in a Camp Oven

Place a small roast and a big roast together in a camp oven. When the small roast is burnt the big roast is ready to eat.

Bush logic

The old shearers cook siept when he wasn't working and worked when he wasn't sleeping!

Joe Watson, 1973

The most popular cooking utensil was the good old billy-can. Stories have been told about it, songs have been sung in praise of it. It is cheap, light and a burden to no one. The billy seems to have originated in the goldrush days when miners consumed a popular French soup known as *bouilli* and, as containers were scarce, the old *bouilli* cans were reused as carrying and

Comfort often meant a campfire, an old pipe, a swag and a nice hearty kangaroo stew. The skin drying on the tree will no doubt be used as a blanket, or maybe our man wants to make another of those roo hats.

cooking containers. Quart-pots, pannikins and jackshays followed as a matter of course. Every bush traveller had a pannikin or two, and a billy-can, and often they were of varying sizes to fit one inside the other to reduce bulk. The most popular-sized billy-cans are the two-quart for tea and four-quart for meat. However, necessity being the mother of invention, many travellers simply used a jam tin with a bit of a handle fashioned from fencing wire. This crude billy was known as the 'Whitely King' from the name of the secretary of the Pastoralists' Union who used scab labour during a shearers' strike — the 'Whitely King' billy was despised by all bushmen.

A special affection was held for the old billy-cans. Men have been known to use their billies in gambling: 'I'll bet my billy boils first,' they would say, and the wise men knew that the older the billy, the quicker it would boil.

Many songs were sung whilst waiting for the billy. Bushmen would often sing the following ditty to the popular tune of 'St Patrick's Day':

Oh, what would you do if the billy boiled over?
Why I'd go and fill it again!

• The Billy of Tea •
(Tune: Bonnie Dundee)

*You may talk of your whisky or talk
  of your beer,
I've something far better awaiting
  me here;
It stands on that fire beneath the
  gum-tree,
And you cannot much lick it — a billy
  of tea.
So fill up your tumbler as high as
  you can,
You'll never persuade me it's not the
  best plan,
To let all the beers and spirits go free
And stick to my darling old billy of tea.*

*I wake in the morning as soon as
  'tis light,
And go to the nosebag to see it's all right,
That the ants on the sugar no mortgage
  have got,
And immediately sling my old black
  billy-pot,*

*And while it is boiling the horses I seek,
And follow them down perhaps as far
  as the creek;
I take off the hobbles and let them
  go free,
And haste to tuck into my billy of tea.*

*And at night when I camp, if the day
  has been warm,
I give each of the horses their tucker
  of corn,
From the two in the pole to the one in
  the lead,
And the billy for each gives a
  comfortable feed;
Then the fire I start and the water I get,
And the corned beef and damper in
  order I set,
But I don't touch the grub, though so
  hungry I be,
I will wait 'till it's ready — the billy
  of tea.*

The Native Companion Songbook, Brisbane, 1889

---

*The Shearer's Song
(Four Little Johnny Cakes)*

*Hurrah for the Lachlan,
Come join in my cheer,
For that's the place to make
   a cheque
At the end of every year,
When you reach a shady bend
Your trouble's at an end,
Campin' for the shearin' in a
   cosy little bend.*

*With me four little Johnny cakes
All nicely cooked,
A nice little codfish
Fresh from the 'ook,
Little round flour-bag
Sittin' on a stump,
Little tea and sugar-bag
Lookin' nice and plump.*

Two verses from the six-verse song
that appeared in the first edition of
A. B. Paterson's *Old Bush Songs*,
Mitchell Library

---

*The babbling brook a shovel
   took
And a damper he unfurled
Another sod! By help me God!
Let loose upon this world!*

Australian Folk Union

Pickled Nasturtiums

Pick the green seeds after the flowers have fallen off. Stems should be about one and a half inches long. Lay stems in salted water for 48 hours then in fresh water for 24 hours. Drain and bottle then add boiling water. They are best eaten after about a month in storage.

There was also a fragment of another song about tea that ran:

*And then there's the price of greens and taters
Oh dear me
It's enough to give a cove the vapours
Oh dear me
To drink colonial tea.*

Quoted in *After Many Days* (1918) by Cuthbert
Featherstonehaugh; this refers to the 1850s.
The author also mentions fictional theatrical
pioneer character Billy Barlow.

Several years ago, when recording the life history of Joe Watson, I arrived with my tape recorder to be met by Joe in an apron. 'I've cooked you up some Johnny cakes,' he told me as he led me into the kitchen. They looked terrific and over a cup of strong brewed tea we ate them hot covered with golden syrup. No Devonshire tea ever tasted so good. Joe gave me the recipe:

These are smaller dampers about the size of the palm of your hand. Take the damper mix and pat the Johnny cakes very thin. Place them directly onto the coals and after a couple of minutes they will swell up and are ready to be turned over. They should be eaten hot and broken by hand. If you want to keep them a while, it is best to put them in an airtight tin otherwise they will be as hard as stone

———— • ————

I remember Old Harry the cook — I don't think anybody ever knew his surname. He was one of the 'best read' men I have had the privilege of knowing. A Shakespearean scholar, he had an excellent knowledge of the arts and sciences. He was always a thorough gentleman, even when as 'high as a kite' on his potato yeast which he brewed ostensibly for bread making. He took a fancy to me when he got on a bender. Periodically he would approach the overseer and inform him that he was 'getting a bit tight in the skin' and wanted to take a few days off (to have a bender). The overseer would negotiate to delay this until a more appropriate time, when a replacement cook could be available, and then he would deliver Harry to the nearest town — after taking the precaution of getting him to leave his bank passbook at the station for safe-keeping. He would then give him a substantial amount of cash which Harry would then commence to 'cut out' on the grog. A week or ten days later we would get an S.O.S. to come and collect Old Harry from the pub. It usually fell to me to take a truck into town to collect him but it wasn't that easy. First I had to get past Old Harry's dog which always took up position outside the room where Harry had fallen into a stupor. The dog wouldn't let anyone approach the room, let alone get near Harry. Strangely enough she would always let me in when he was in this state, but would ignore me when Harry was sober and on his feet. I would pick up Old Harry and carry him out to the truck where the dog would continually lick his face to either keep the flies off or sober him up, whilst I negotiated with the publican to redeem Harry's false teeth which would be in a brown paper bag in the cash register! When his money ran out he always pawned his teeth to cover 'just a couple more drinks'. I would then buy a bottle of O.P. rum and over the next few days would always allow Harry to have a tot at regular intervals — getting him on his feet with prairie oysters of raw egg and rum. Harry was one of the best and we regarded him so highly, when sober, that no one minded his occasional benders.

From the manuscripts of Alan Lindsay Arnold Brownlee, forwarded to the author in 1972

There were several well known women cooks, but as the cook had to prepare all the firewood and get up an hour before 'sparrow fart' it was a very hard life and few women elected to stay. The Chinese were also popular as station or travelling cooks; many of today's country Chinese restaurants would have been started by station cooks and their families with broad Australian accents and a locally adapted Chinese menu that seems to owe more to the shearing shed than the traditions of China.

Like most Australians, the cook was known by his nickname. Sometimes it would be an affectionate 'Old Baitlayer' or 'Belly-whinger'. Sometimes the nickname would refer to a specialty dish like 'Hot Bum' the curry maker or 'The Baker' known for his breads and pies. Bad-tempered cooks fared much worse — 'Grizzle-Guts', 'Stone Face', 'Bowel Twister', and 'Silent Knight', so called because he rarely uttered a word. Most old time bush workers can tell horror stories about station or camp cooks and the sometimes odd tucker produced in the 'Bedourie oven', particularly their interpretation of what was generally known as the 'complete bush baked dinner' — stew.

———— • ————

Anyone who remembered the Wimmera country in South Australia will remember a noted old character called Cadger Jimmy who used to bestow his valuable company in regular rotation on all stations within a five-hundred-mile radius, until he became a recognised bush institution. Indeed, it was of little use trying to stand out against what he seemingly had got to consider his vested interests — namely, the free run of the men's huts and a supply of 'cold scran' to carry him through to the next station. He was such a favourite with the men and his arrival was always hailed with so much satisfaction that even if the boss refused him tucker he would certainly be smuggled into the hut and fed just the same.

His great popularity was owing to his jovial disposition and the number of spicy yarns, comic ditties and pithy sayings with which he was replete and which made his advent a welcome break in the monotony of station life. One night I approached the hut and there was cold silence and then the full voice of the old reprobate broke into a song which he called 'The Wallaby Track'. I afterwards took the trouble to copy down the words.

J. C. F. Johnson, *Memoirs*, 1873

Bush Stew

2 oxtails, 1 sliced onion, 3 diced potatoes, 1 cup cooked rice, salt and pepper, 3 cups of brown stock, 2 chopped tomatoes, 2 sliced carrots, 1 tablespoon Worcestershire sauce

Cut the oxtails into pieces at joints and soak in salted water for a couple of hours. Drain them and brown them in dripping. Put pieces in deep pan with stock, onions etc, and cook for 4 hours on a low heat. Add diced spuds and cook a further half an hour. Take a deep breath and hoe in.

Joe Watson, 1974

A portable cookhouse with the cook's sleeping quarters attached. If you look closely into the picture you will see a hand-mincing machine attached to the fold-out counter — mince was a staple in the cook's repertoire. This photograph from around 1925 shows the cookie on Clifton station during the chaff-cutting season.

We had a cook out at Wilagra Station and I swear he never ever washed. He was known as Greasy Simmo and he was a shocking man and his hide was always greasy. The blokes used to say that you couldn't even look at him because your eyes would just slip off him. He was that greasy!

Another cook was known as Blue Stew Lou. He earned his nickname several years earlier because of an incident where some shearers had dropped a Reckitt's Blue bag into one of his stew pots. Apparently he had been on a bit of a bender and for weeks he kept serving up the same stew. The men said he never ever cleaned the bottom of the pot and that he just kept adding to it every day. When they dropped the bag Lou saw the joke and announced to all and sundry that he had a surprise for their evening meal. 'Blue Stew!' He declared.

• Jim the Cadger on the Wallaby Track •
(Tune: The Cures)

You want to know my title and likewise who I am?
Then hark and I will tell you and I won't tell you a cram
My name is Jim the Cadger, I'm a downy cove, you see,
'Hard graft', it ain't my fancy for it somehow don't suit me.

Chorus
So trampers gather 'round and I'll tell you in a crack,
How to work the stations when you're on the wallaby track.

Yes, I'm a jovial cadger, I roves the country 'round
And goes to all the stations where I hope work won't be found!
The men's hut then I enter, and just the night to stay,
And the grub I prigs at breakfast, will last me through the day.
But sometimes cooks is crusty and they tell you that the cove
Says trampers are too plentiful, give them no grub, by jove,
You may doss down in the woolshed and sleep there for the night.

But as far as mutton and damper why he can't give you a bite.

If slewed then at the station, streak for some shepherd's hut
'Ses you, 'Since early morning, I ain't had a bite or sup,'
Says he, 'Here's mutton and damper and on the fire there's tea,
So flash your dover hearty for there's heaps for you and me.'

So Sunday, Monday, Tuesday, I jog upon my way,
With a little banje or whaling just to fill up the day
But regular at sundown I on some station drop,
And I tell you it isn't often that when I'm asked to stop.

Now having sung my ditty, I may as well shut up shop,
For I ain't got no more to say, I've told you quite enough
About how to do the squatters as I promised sometime back,
And how to work the stations when on the wallaby track.

From a soft-covered booklet entitled *Christmas on Carringa*
by J. C. Johnson, published in Adelaide in 1873

Buggers on the Coals

Now I'm living in retirement, and I live a life of ease,
Catching up on all my hobbies just exactly as I please,
But when my thoughts they wander to my droving days of old
I can't say that I hanker for those buggers on the coals!

From Cec Cory, collected in Cairns, 1972 by Wendy Lowenstein

One of the skills of bush cooking was the art of firemaking. The coals had to be the right temperature to cook pastry and damper. You also had to know your timber because certain wood burns quicker or hotter than others. You also had to know the feel of the wind and whether it would change direction mid fire. Water knowledge was also vital especially ways of cleaning muddy water to prevent 'bugs' that caused dysentery or the 'Barcoo' runs. The cookie had a travelling kitchen that included specially made camp ovens designed to cook bread, stews, sauces and the like. The cook had to clean and repair where necessary. On top of all this the cook was expected to be a bit of a 'character' and able to either spin a yarn or sing a song. It was a busy life!

• Bushtershire Sauce •
Many Australians missed the taste of English condiments and sauces so they made their own. This is a version of Worcestershire sauce: Boil the following ingredients together for about half an hour then allow to cool: 1 gal of vinegar, 3 lb treacle, 1 bottle of anchovy sauce, 2 oz cloves, 1 oz of cayenne pepper, 2 oz garlic and salt.

I love these recipes that call for something like 'a gallon of vinegar'; we are now so used to convenience shopping and cooking that the very thought of cooking in large quantities is amusing. There was obviously no choice in the

A giant ants' nest turned into the perfect bush cook's oven. Our man probably turned out some fine pastries and stews from this ingenious device.

old days for, if a vegetable or fruit was in season, cooks and settlers prepared as much as possible. Storage was a real problem and all manner of bush refrigeration was invented. The most famous is the typical cooler room, a small storage room with a tank on top that allowed water to continually seep through the charcoal walls which would, in turn, keep the contents of the room at a steady temperature. Slain meat, smoked meats, preserves and extra rations were all kept in these cooler rooms. The simple 'meat safe' that hung from the nearby tree was another ingenious method of keeping the food from the animals, insects and direct sunshine. Food preserving was a fact of life. The popularity of the famous Fowler's Vacola food preserving system is well documented with its big cooking vat, strainers, temperature indicator, hundreds of bottles and rubber-lined bottle caps.

Quandong Jam

This fruit is only found on the inland plains of Australia. Remove the kernels and add about three times its own bulk in brown sugar and allow to boil at a low heat for as long as it likes. Allow to cool and the jam is ready to eat. If you wish to keep the quandong fruit for a long time you can bury them in sand and they will ripen very slowly.

Green Tomato Jam

You will need about eight pounds of green tomatoes cut into slices. Add one pint of water and ½ lb of preserved ginger and boil until cooked. Add 6 lb of sugar and the juice of three lemons then boil some more until it looks and tastes right.

Mutton Batter

6 oz flour, 2 eggs; 1 pint milk; ½ lb of mutton, salt and seasoning. Cut the mutton into pieces and place them in a greased dish. Beat the eggs well and add the milk. Gradually work this into the mixed flour, salt and seasoning then pour over the meat and bake for one and a half hours.

Not only did the mighty sheep contribute to the early success of the Australian economy, he also contributed to our cuisine. Entire books were written with titles like *Clever Things to do with Mutton* and *Recipes for Ewe*.

Boiled Leg of Mutton

This favourite Australian dish is quite simple to prepare. Boil one leg of mutton with salt and pepper. Occasionally remove the scum and the secret is that the dish must be cooked but not overcooked. End of recipe!

Sheep's Trotters

Sheep's feet were generally thrown away in Australia, although they make an excellent dish stewed, and are delicate for jelly. For trotters clean and boil then soak in salt and vinegar for a day and dry them ready for frying. Dip in egg and breadcrumbs and fry until brown.

Mutton Macaroni

Put a few steams of mutton on to simmer for an hour, with a quarter of a pound of macaroni, and a little water; season with pepper and salt and cayenne pepper. Add some chutney and a tablespoon of vinegar. Cook and eat.

• The Seven 'Goods' of Mutton •

1ST.	The mutton must be good	**5TH.**	Who must be in a good temper
2ND.	Must have been kept a good time	**6TH.**	The mashed turnips must be good
3RD.	Must be boiled by a good fire	**7TH.**	The eater must have a good appetite
4TH.	By a good cook		

Files of Australian Folklore Unit

My favourite bush recipe is still the following for roasted mutton: Build a fire and shove the mutton on top till it's cooked. Set the table and eat!

Today the bush cook operates in a modern kitchen and even has apprentices to 'do the dirty work'. Many of these outback cooks are really chefs, both male and female, who are contracted to dish up exotic meals to the workers. Today's shearer is more likely to dine on French onion soup, quiche with cos lettuce salad and a sweet of profiterolles.

• Bush Method of Catching Fish •

On a couple of occasions we caught a considerable number of fish whilst at Buckinguy station. Most of the waterholes in the Naree Creek were dried up and the remainder very low. About three miles from our old shed were a few holes containing about three feet of water and on two occasions we dragged these holes for fish. We got some wire netting sufficient to reach across the waterholes and we tied the wire to poles, then a couple of us would wade in and remove all the sticks and rubbish and, at the same time, stir up the water to make it all muddy. We'd then spread the net and drag it across the hole, forcing the fish up one end and then we simply scooped them into buckets. Some of the boys just grabbed the codfish and threw them onto the grass but they put a bit of a fight and caused cuts to the hands. By the end of the day we had about eighty big codfish weighing from 1 lb to 10 lb.

P. J. Gresser, *Memoirs*, Mitchell Library Manuscripts, Sydney
Buckinguy is about sixty kilometres from Nyngan in the central west of New South Wales and the year was 1924

No fancy fishing rods here, but there's a good chance this old bloke knew what to expect for dinner. His mate, engrossed in the weekly news, has a couple of beers at the ready but isn't in that much of a hurry. There's no hurry in hard times.

The army cooks weren't much better than the early bush cooks; they were often the very same 'bastards' who had swapped the shearing shed for the army barrack. There is a common saying that 'an army marches on its stomach'; this probably explains the 'stick to the ribs' approach to army cooking. Army cooks also copped such nicknames as 'Slops', 'Slushy', 'Snags' and 'Crippen', the last after the notorious British poisoner early this century. Mass-produced food is rarely appetising and many biting ditties came out of the Australian war experience. The themes are common ones: 'The officer's eating better food than the privates', 'Not bloody stew again', 'Bully-beef', 'Porridge so hard it should be used as ammunition', etc.

Overheard in the barracks: 'What sort of cook is the new bloke?' to which the disgruntled reply came: 'Just!' Like the bush cook, the army cook had a tough life. He had to be first to emerge in the dead hours of early morning with the duty of producing edible tucker from almost inedible rations. There would be no thanks from the men, who more often than not used the cook as a scapegoat for the hard routine of being at war.

It seems that there was only one thing worse than eating camp food — having to live off World War II ration packs cooked in the dixie, the soldiers' equivalent of the billy-can. Each K-ration kit had tinned camp pie, soup mix, a sweet and biscuits as hard as nails. As school cadets we often dined on these rations for a night; the thought of endless weeks of these rations is enough to make anyone a conscientious objector.

Army tea and cocoa were also subject to thriving folklore; the number one belief was that the army brass used these drinks to administer 'bromides' to the soldiers to reduce their sexual desires.

Favourite Australian recipes fit for the bush, the barracks or the boarding house:

Irish Stew

Take two pounds of mutton and cut into fair pieces, and four pounds of potatoes and cut them in half; six onions peeled and sliced. Put a layer of the potatoes on the bottom of the pot and then some of the meat and onions, a small spoonful of pepper and some salt. The stew must simmer and not boil for about two hours.

Bread and Butter Pudding

Wash and clean two ounces of currants, get ready five or six layers of bread and butter, put the bread in the dish, and between the layers put the currants, and all over pour a generous custard. Bake for three-quarters of an hour.

This anonymous ditty was sung in the Djakarta prison camp in 1942.

Screw 'em all, screw 'em all,
The long and the short and
*   the tall,*
Screw all the guards and each
*   bow-leg Jap,*
Screw all the cooks and their
*   flamin' rice pap.*
When we're going away from
*   it all,*
And there's no guard to screech
*   and to bawl,*
They can stuff their pick axes
Right up their jack-asses,
So cheer up me lads screw
*   'em all.*

Quoted in *G String Jesters* by Norman Carter, a military revue of the 1940s

'There's far too many flies
about the cookhouse!'
'Yessir — how many should
there be?'

The women of Henty, NSW, sending their men to the first world war with a full stomach of Bushell's tea and homemade cakes.

When you hear a daily call to meals, be it a gong, bell or bugle, you eventually start to imagine words to fit the tune. The following ditties were collected from a slim, soft-covered booklet, titled *Songs for Soldiers* by Captain George Taylor (1913) in the Mitchell Library, Sydney.

> ***Officer's first call to dress dinner:***
> *Now officers with your might,*
> *Just polish up your appetite.*

> ***And the second call to the officer's***
> ***mess went:***
> *The waiters wait, now don't be late,*
> *For moments fast are fleeting,*
> *The menu's fine, so when you dine,*
> *You'll get that feeling so divine,*
> *That comes from pleasant eating!*

DIGGER

DESSERT
PRUNES

The theme of food so tough that it could be used for ammunition is a recurring one and was at least one way to get back at the cooks. Variants of the following parody on 'Christmas Day in the Poorhouse' were common.

> *It was Christmas Day in the barracks*
> *The cook had brought in the duff*
> *Up spoke a sturdy soldier*
> *Who said it was too bloody tough!*
> *'We don't want your Christmas pudding*
> *Send it out the front for the guns*
> *Ram it down the neck of a cannon*
> *And fire it straight at the Huns.'*

From Mrs Rollinson, Brisbane, 1973

Soldiers having dinner at the Bilambil settlement in 1920. Note the tin of Arnott's biscuits on the table and the ever-present enamel mugs, destined to take a layer of skin off eager drinkers' lips.

All soldiers live on bread
  and jam
They like it better than eggs
  and ham
Early in the morning
You hear the corporal say:
'Stew, stew, stew, stew,
Stew for dinner today!'

From George Fahey, 1973

'Now, for cream puffs you must have a very delicate touch.'

"*Across the board our hands go forth
In comradeship renewed,
To steadfast hands, that proved the worth
Of Faith and Fortitude.*"

G.I.

———

"*Fallen Comrades*" . . . . The Chairman
"*Roll Call*" . . . . A. H. Hocking, Esq.
"*THE KING*" E. Hilmer Smith, Esq. (Chairman)
"*THE BANK*" . . . . A. D. M. Catto, Esq.

RESPONSE

SIR ERNEST COOPER RIDDLE (Govenor).
H. T. ARMITAGE, Esq. (Deputy Govenor).

M.C. . . . . A. H. Hocking, Esq. (36th Battn.)

———

ARTISTS:

F. CROSS, Esq. . . . . (17th Battn.)
B. HARROW, Esq. . . . . . (R.F.C.)
GEO. BROWN, Esq. . . . (11th Field Amb.)
BUGLER: Sgt. J. E. MAGEE (Cav. M.G.C.)

PIANIST:

FRANK DONOVAN . . . . (A.F.A.)

Menu by Geoff. Baker.

• Tune: The Quartermaster's Store •

We are the P.O.W.s pouring out our woes,
On a dreadful diet and this how it goes:
There is rice, rice, mouldy rotten rice,
Nothing more, nothing more,
There are eggs, eggs, growing little legs,
Let's throw them at their shaven heads.

Chorus
They are so blind they cannot see,
This is not enough for you and me,
And we're all so damned hungry.

There is spinach, spinach, the grubs
thrive in it,
Nothing more, nothing more,
There are spuds, spuds, most of them
are duds,
Let's throw them at the yellow thugs.

There is pork, pork, a bit of skinny pork,
Nothing more, nothing more,
There is yak, yak, yak we cannot hack,
Let's throw this tough stuff back.

There are leeks, leeks, oh how it reeks,
Nothing more, nothing more,
There is cabbage, cabbage, rescued from
the garbage,
Only good enough for the yellow baggage.

Final Chorus
They are so blind they do not know,
How tired of this we all do grow,
And we want to go home right now!

Written by two sisters, Val and Ray Smith, in
Palembang prison camp, Malaya in 1941. Quoted in
White Coolies, a war diary by Betty Jeffery, 1958

Community Songs

:: FOR THE ::

11th. Anzac Dinner

Australia's sons, let us rejoice,
For we are young and free:
We've golden soil and wealth for toil,
Our home is girt by sea;
Our lands abound in nature's gifts
Of beauty rich and rare;
In history's page, let every stage
Advance Australia fair
CHORUS:
In joyful steains then let us sing
Advance Australia fair

Cooking for the troops is now a high-tech occupation that includes high nutritional dietary planning through to the most effective freeze drying for the new-style ration pack. In the *Australian* magazine (December, 1990) Chris Forbes-Ewan, of the Physiology and Nutrition Department of Defence Materials Research Laboratory in Scottsdale, Tasmania commented that, 'Morale depends so heavily on food, a decent meal is often the only thing you have to look forward to, for days and weeks on end. If you have a crook cook then morale drops — if you can't look forward to good food, then what else is there?'

The current Australian army ration pack is quite impressive, and the twenty-four-hour menu includes ham and egg, beef and vegetables, freeze-dried rice, peaches, biscuits, plum jam, cereal, cheese, chocolate, curry powder, chewing gum, butter concentrate, butterscotch, condensed milk, two tea bags, sugar, salt, fruit drink powder, matches, tin opener, rubber band, toilet paper, scouring pad with soap. Everything but the kitchen sink and a condom!

Save-All Pudding

Put bread scraps in a saucepan with a little milk, break in three eggs and add three ounces of sugar, a little nutmeg, ginger and allspice and stew all together. This pudding may be baked or boiled. Throw in some currants if available.

Baked Rice Pudding

Boil six ounces of rice, and, when done, put in a dish and pour a ready made custard on top. Bake quickly for twenty minutes.

'What sort of cook is he? Just a cook!' This station cook is ready for business with the tables laid and even a homely touch of serrated paper table cloth.

Boarding-house cuisine, like army catering, had a reputation for being big on stodge. Music hall monologues and songs are full of jokes about boarding house food being large on helpings and small on flavour. Ask any school boarder about food and they usually groan in reply as memories of mashed pumpkin, chokos, stews, sausages and macaroni pies return. Such food tended to be overcooked, oversalted and poorly presented. It also produced its fair share of folklore.

Oh, love is a very funny thing
It affects both young and old
It's like a plate of boarding-house hash
And many's the young man that it sold

It makes you feel like a freshwater eel
Causes your head to swell
You'll lose your mind, 'cause love is blind
And it will empty your pocket-book as well.

'The Bald-headed End of the Broom' as sung by Herb Green, St Lucia, Qld, 1973

Tapioca and sago were extremely popular in Australia but both seem to have disappeared from favour. Maybe they were too closely associated with the lean times of the 1930s Depression, or maybe leftovers from the boarding house days. Sydney jewellery designer Ray Griffiths once reintroduced me to the delights of the sago pudding and then asked his mother for the family recipes.

Lemon Sago

2 oz sago, 1 pint cold water, 1 tablespoon golden syrup, sugar, juice and grated rind of one lemon

Mix and simmer all ingredients until sago is clear, serve hot or cold with custard or cream.

Mrs Betty Griffiths, Adelaide, SA

Passionfruit and Sago Shape

4 oz sago, 1 pint water, ½ cup of sugar, 1 cup of passionfruit pulp

Soak the sago in water then boil until clear. Add the passionfruit and sugar then pour into a wet mould. Turn out when cold and serve with custard or cream.

Mrs Betty Griffiths, Adelaide, SA

• Sago Plum Pudding •

3 tablespoons of sago, ½ cup sugar, 1 cup soft white breadcrumbs, 1 cup milk, 1 cup raisins or sultanas, 1 egg, ½ teaspoon cinnamon, 3 oz butter, ½ teaspoon bicarbonate soda, pinch of salt, 1 tablespoon golden syrup.

Wash sago well and soak overnight in the milk. Cream together the butter and sugar and add the beaten egg and the golden syrup. Dissolve the bicarbonate soda in the milk and sago and add to the mixture, stir in the salt, sultanas, cinnamon and breadcrumbs. Pour into a well greased mould. Cover and boil for three hours.

Mrs Betty Griffiths, Adelaide, SA

• The Cook's Revenge •

Once I took a job of cooking,
For some poddy-dodging cows,
But of all the little jobs I had,
It took the cake for rows.

The bloody meat was gone bad,
And the cake it was a sod,
For the damper had gone ropey,
It was, so help me Bob.

The tea it looked like water,
And the pudding just as bad,
And every time we forked it on,
It made us fellows mad.

One day I thought, 'I'll square things!'
And let them see no mug was I,
So I mixed some sniftin' pea soup,
To make them fellows cry.

Half a tin of curry,
To give the stuff a grip,
And half at tin of pepper,
To make them fellows shit.

And half a tin of cow dung,
Singed to make it look like toast,
The stink of it would knock you down,
Like Jesus Holy Ghost!

So the stockmen came in early,
If no tucker — Look out for us,
'Just hop in here you stockmen boys,
For I'll bring some soup to light.'

So the plate full each they took,
By cripes it tastes all right,
But nothing like the second helping,
To make them bastards shite.

They shit upon the tables,
They shit upon the floor,
The rotten dirty bastards —
They never asked for more.

So I snatched my time
And wandered down the line,
So if you're looking for a first-class cook —
I'm waiting for a job!

From Arthur Croydon, recorded by Ron Edwards in Cairns, 1970,
and published in *Australian Folk Songs*

'Anyone else got anything
to say about my cookin'?'

Savoury Chops

4 shoulder chops, 1 tablespoon sugar, 2 tablespoons flour, 2 tablespoons vinegar, 2 tablespoons tomato sauce, 1 tablespoon rice, 1 onion, 1 teaspoon salt, ⅛ teaspoon pepper, ¼ teaspoon ground ginger, ¼ teaspoon curry powder, ¼ teaspoon mustard, ¼ teaspoon mixed spice, water

Place chops in casserole dish and cover with chopped onion and rice. Mix remaining ingredients and place over chops. Add enough water to cover. Stand for an hour and then cook at 175°F for about two hours.

Mrs J. Moore, Bexley, NSW

'Leftovers' in Australia usually meant 'Bubble and Squeak' which is a name for just about anything refried and served up with a couple of eggs. Many old-timers swear by this as the best hangover cure, especially if doused with a liberal amount of good old Father's Favourite sauce.

• Bubble and Squeak •

Slightly fry some cold shredded leftover meat. Corned beef is excellent. Add cold shredded cabbage and pepper and salt to taste and fry for a few minutes. Serve with fried eggs and sauce.

• Sheep Kidney Casserole •

Skin five sheep kidneys and cut into pieces ¼ in thick, removing the core. Slice 1 onion and two carrots and dredge these and the kidneys with seasoned flour. Fry lightly in 2 tablespoons of butter until golden brown. Drain and place in a 20 cm casserole dish. Make a gravy in the pan, using ¼ teaspoon of dry mustard and stock. Pour over kidneys etc cover and bake for one hour until tender.

Mrs J. Moore, Bexley, NSW

• Tomato Soup Cake •

2 cups of sifted flour, 4 tsp baking powder, 2 well beaten eggs, ½ tsp bicarb. soda, ½ tsp cinnamon, nutmeg, ½ cup butter, ½ tsp ground cloves, 1 cup seedless raisins, 1 cup sugar, 1½ cups of tomato soup

Sift together the flour, baking powder, soda, and spices. Clean and chop raisins and roll in a small amount of flour. Cream butter and gradually add sugar, then eggs, mixing thoroughly. Add flour mixture alternatively with soup (tinned and thick soup is best). Stir until smooth then fold in raisins. Pour into two 8-inch sandwich tins (greased and floured), bake in a moderate oven about 30–35 minutes. Cool on a cake cooler. When cold they may be joined with whipped cream, and covered with vanilla or lemon icing.

Mrs Powell, Albany, WA

Other favoured recipes include roast lamb, corned beef hash, lamb's fry, milk braised tripe, thick pea soup, cold ox tongue and, of course, rissoles with onion gravy sauce.

Whether in a cattle camp, shearing shed, army barracks or boarding house, the poor old cookie seems to have had an uphill battle in gaining respect from his or her clientele. Could these 'dark sides' of our food history have played a part in shaping our ongoing attitudes to dining and to cuisine? Is it possible that we all have a little bit of 'bushwacker' along with our Australian sense of humour? I think so!

3

Necessity the Mother of Invention

We're on the susso now
We can't afford a cow
We live in a tent
We pay no rent
We're on the susso now

Depression ditty

WHEN food was short, particularly during the economic Depressions of the 1890s and 1930s, we 'made do' with what we could scrape up. As a nation we have never known famine, though many Australians caught in hard economic times relieved the pangs of hunger with sandwiches of bread and dripping, soup made of potato peelings and a weekly stew of rabbit. No fancy recipes came out of recession; there wasn't much that even the most talented chef could devise to smarten up the taste of bread and dripping.

The Depression of the 1890s was mainly a rural economic collapse that affected the working man. These were the days when disillusioned farmers just walked off their property to leave the troubles to the dingoes and the crows. Men, women and even children joined the thousands of travelling people who tramped from town to town seeking work and living off a meagre sustenance payment. These were the days of the swagmen, bagmen, sundowners, knot-carriers and the hungry miles — the land of milk and honey had turned sour.

These were cruel times for Australia for, up to the late 1880s, it was generally believed that nothing really could go wrong with Australia's economy. We were an export force to be reckoned with and we were also of the opinion that we were living in 'God's own' land. Despite individual poverty the feelings of nationalism reinforced our general opinion of colonial strength and 'home on the sheep's back'. The Depression of the 1890s well and truly shattered those dreams! One can well imagine that songs like 'The Farmer Feeds Them All' would gain widespread popularity as the population painfully realised that the farmer indeed was 'the man' and that we had almost slaughtered the goose that laid the golden egg!

As the Depression worsened, the road travellers grew into an army, tramping from town to town. They set up tent cities and every river bend and bridge became a mass campsite. Men, women and children existed on the bare minimum, cheered by radical talk of revolution and socialism. Although food was often shared it was more often eaten in secret; there was a general attitude of 'every man for himself'. Tea, however, was always shared, and the water was nearly always on the boil. The Depression

Although we've plenty of bees and cows,
This land's not milk and honey,
For the cows are all in parliament
And the b's have got all the money!

Early political ditty collected by the author

'Twas done without reason, for, leaving the season,
No squatter could stand such a rub!
For it's useless to squat when the rents are so hot
That you can't save the price of your grub!

From *The Broken Down Squatter*, by Charles Flower

• T H E   F a r m e r   F e e d s   T h e m   A l l •

The king may rule o'er land or sea,
The lord may live right loyally,
The sailor roam across the ocean wide,
But this or that what ere befall;
The farmer must feed them all.

The writer thinks; the poet sings,
The craftsman fashions wondrous
*   things.*
The doctor heals, the lawyer pleads,
The miner follows the precious leads:
But the farmer he must feed them all.

The merchant he must buy and sell,
The teacher do his duty well,
But men may toil through busy days,
Or men may stroll through pleasant
*   ways,*

From king to beggar what'er befalls:
The farmer he must feed them all.

The farmer's trade is one of worth,
He's partner with the sky and earth,
He's partner with the sun and rain,
And no man loses from his gain;
And men may rise and men may fall:
But the farmer he must feed them all.

God bless the man who sows the wheat,
Who finds its milk, fruit and meat,
May his purse be heavy, his heart
*   be light,*
His cattle, corn and ale go right,
God bless the seeds his hands let fall:
For the farmer he must feed them all.

A very old item from the Wrench family scrapbook in the Mitchell Library dated 1890.
The family lived in the Hill End/Bathurst area of New South Wales.

That woman is about to pour boiling tea all over her hand and her friend will be completely cross-eyed if someone doesn't remove that tea-cosy from her head. This scene, from a picnic at La Perouse in 1916, shows the limited fare used in alfresco dining.

coincided with the great shearing industry strike of the 1890s. And these men knew about survival and such mass anger tended to knot the stomach where determination outweighed the need to eat. The strike also bonded the shearers together and the philosophy of every man for himself became one for all and all for one.

Much has been written about the history of tea in Australia, and it is indeed a noble one. The shearers shared tea, the drovers and bullockies longed for the

setting sun and a strong mug of it, and in the cities factory workers were stopping for a tea break and housewives brewed the mid-morning 'cuppa'.

Generations of Australians have defined the art of tea drinking. By necessity, and with a good spoonful of rebellion we soon abandoned the British traditions associated with tea drinking. Fine china, tea pots and cucumber sandwiches were almost useless in the bush when all a bloke wanted was a pannikin of tea. The tea itself was imported, apparently costing very little and uniform in quality.

Traditionally the bushman made tea by boiling clean (with any luck) water in a billy-can and throwing in a generous handful of tea when the water came to the boil. The next step was to make the tea sink to the bottom and several methods were employed. Some men added a couple of gum-leaves, claiming that they made the tea sink; others insisted that the leaves would always separate when the sides of the billy-can were given seven or eight firm taps with a stick. Some bushies stirred the tea with a twig whilst others recommended swinging the boiled tea around with a circular motion so that the laws of gravity forced the tea to the bottom of the billy-can. (I must say that I have spent nearly twenty-five years drinking bush-style tea, and I'll be blowed if there is any way to make the leaves sink. A mouthful of tea-leaves seems par for the bush!) Experienced bush tea drinkers know that the leaves are part of the ritual and the best way to avoid their bitter taste is to simply blow them away as you sip the tea.

Most bush tea drinkers drank their tea strong. It was widely referred to as 'jack the painter' because of the stain that the strong brew left around the mouth. It is said that the best tea is 'strong enough for the spoon to stand up by itself'. Some tea drinkers added sugar and, where available, milk. The image of the sturdy bush worker leaning against a gum tree and sipping a

mug of tea was successfully adopted by the tea merchant James Inglis and Co. Ltd., for the Billy Tea advertising campaign.

The Australian population brewed other teas; even in pioneering days, the remedial benefits of herbal teas were acknowledged. It should be pointed out that these were consumed for medicinal purposes rather than for pleasure. Red sage leaf tea was used as a blood purifier, goldenrod was for backache, red clover tea for cancers, foxglove and broom for dropsy. If one had a craving for alcohol, the cure was a tea of gold-thread root. It was also believed that inferior tea caused diabetes and too strong a blend caused sight to dim. (This wisdom, published in a booklet *Golden Recipes — Knowledge is Power*, was sold on newstands and by mail order from the 1890s through to about the 1930s.)

The sundowners, those travellers of the road, refined tea drinking, and every swag contained the 'makings' of billy, tea and sugar. The 1890s and 1930s had many similarities as lean years', and much of the history and folklore is intertwined. When I think of bush tea I always go back to that marvellous extract from Steele Rudd's *On Our Selection* (1899) where Mother is complaining about not having money enough to buy tea and Dad goes through this extraordinary performance: 'We couldn't very well go without tea, so Dad showed Mother how to make a new kind. He roasted a slice of bread on the fire till it was like a black coal, then poured the boiling water over it and let it draw well. Dad said it had a capital flavour — he liked it.'

———— • ————

There was a special way to carry a swag, that was one thing that my mate, Cock Robbin, taught me. He said, 'Cor blimey! How long have you been carrying the knot?' I said, 'Not long but long enough!' He said, 'I don't think so — you've got to roll it up tight and carry it high on your shoulders with the billy swinging neat with the sweat roll, your towel, as the carry strap. If you don't roll it right it will be the death of you and make it bloody impossible to jump a train.' I tell you that after he fixed my swag I could go twenty five miles a day without a problem.

Oh, there were all sorts of ways to get tucker. When we were really desperate we would fiddle the general stores. Cock Robbin was a real professional swagman and had a technique that always resulted in rations. He'd go into a store and be extra polite. 'Good morning sir, lovely day isn't it, sir,' and as he bowed and blurted he would accidentally knock over the biggest display of tinned food, it would be tinned peaches or salmon or something he fancied. 'Oh, goodness me!' he'd shout, 'Let me fix this mess, I'm dreadfully sorry, sir.' He'd fix it all up and quickly excuse himself. Of course he always grabbed at least half a dozen cans for his tucker bag!

It was tea that kept body and soul together. It's amazing how long you can go without actual hard tucker if you can still boil up the billy. We always had our tea strong as paint and liked it that way.

During the hungry years of the 1890s it was common for bagmen and swagmen to cadge supplies off station owners, and everyone had his own method of cadging. I once heard of a professional swagman who used to try and embarrass the station women into more rations. One day this cove sauntered up to a station homestead, knocked firmly on the door and stood there with his head bowed and hands behind his back. When the woman of the house answered the door she sharply eyed him up and down and snapped, 'Yes! What do you want?' 'Well, missus,' he whinged, 'I've been on the track for many months and I was wondering if you could spare me some margarine.' And as he said this he brought his hand around and shoved a dried-up old cow patty at her, repeating, 'Could ya spare me some margarine?' Well, she looked at him and then grabbed the meadowcake which she flung into the yard saying, 'You poor old devil — you go around to the back of the house, there's some fresh ones around there!'

From Bartholomew Saggers, who lived through the Depression of the 1930s as a professional swagman

The Swagman's Curse

There ain't no work in Bourke
Damn all at Blackall
No lucre at Eucha
Things are crook at Tallarook
Might get a feed at the Tweed
No feedin' at Eden
Might get a berth in Perth
In gaol in Innisfail
Got the arse at Bulli Pass.

Traditional Depression ditty

Judging by his peek-a-boo shoes, this swagman has already tramped more than his fair share of tracks, but at least he has a spare pair hanging from his kit. Note the well-balanced swag, so important if one wanted to last the distance.

We had another professional swagman in our team and his name was Cockeye Burns. His specialty was chicken dinners. He had this technique where he could leave camp early in the morning taking a sugar bag and he always returned with one or two prime chooks. I went with him one morning and he had me shaking like a tapioca pudding. He used to creep into the henhouse and kept clucking all the time, he used to say he was talking to them, he'd hold the sugar bag in front of the chicken and then tickle its bum and whammo the next thing you know the chicken is in the bloody bag!

Cockeye Burns was a cook too, and he used to work on the stations. One night he caught a carpet snake and cooked it up for the camp. It was a big bugger and tasted terrific. He cooked it over the coals in cunjevoi leaves and clay. He made a damper for us once but the blokes reckoned he had used sheep droppings instead of raisins and we'd never let him cook for us again.

Bart Saggers, Brisbane, Qld, 1973

As a diversion from the truth, many travellers of the road romanticised their bleak lifestyle. The swagman called himself a 'roads scholar' or 'professional traveller' and pictured himself as someone who had elected to travel the road to seek fame and education (fortune was not included!).

• The Two Professional Hums •
(Tune: Jolly Lads Are We)

Come all you jovial fellows and listen
to me, chums,
And I'll relate to you, my boys, of two
professional hums,
Who travelled England, Ireland, all
over Scotland too,
And took an oath at Bendigo no more
work they would do.
No more work they would do boys,
Troll old army doughboys,
Humming a drink where e'er we go,
Sing fol the right o-o.

Chorus
For we are hums and jolly good chums,
We live like royal Turks,
And if we've luck we'll hum our cheques,
And shoot the man who works.

I asked a lady the other day for
something for to eat,
A little piece of bacon or a little piece
of meat,

A little piece of turkey or a little piece
of ham,
Half a dozen loaves of bread and a
bucket full of jam.
Or anything at all, Ma'am, for we are
bloody starvin'
Anything to help a couple of jokers on
their way:

A farmer asked us the other day if we
would go to graft,
Says I: 'What is the work?' He says,
'A cutting of the chaff.'
I said, 'What is the payment?' 'A dollar
and a half for some,'
I said, 'Go shoot yourself, 'cause we
would rather hum,
Than work upon the harvest and let the
cocky starve us,'
Humming a drink where e'er we go,
Sing fol the righty-o-o . . .

Harry Chaplin, recorded Broken Hill, NSW, 1974

As people travelled around the country they learned the tricks of the trade, said Bartholomew Saggers, who claimed to be a 'professional swagman'. He reckoned he could 'cadge rations out of an empty swag' and because of his skills he had been dubbed 'the Great Australian Bite'.

We used to carry rations of five of flour, two of beef, half of sugar and half of tea. That made it the 5, 2 and 1 and we'd call it the 'Five Double R'. You know, a doubler, the half and half! There was a game you had to use to cadge rations, and you soon learn that not every town's full of angels and not all towns are full of villains. You'll always find an in-between and if you've got the technique you'd come away with a full belly. The wives of station owners were often very good. They had a lot of sympathy for the knot-carriers and often you'd be asked to do odd jobs in return for rations. I remember one cove asked me if I could kill a sheep in exchange for a couple of nights accommodation. I replied that I hadn't killed one before, but I'd knock it over that much that he'd take a bloody long time to get over it! — He gave me the job saying, 'You'll go a long way, son.'

Bartholomew Saggers, recorded by Warren Fahey, Brisbane, Qld, 1973

Bart Saggers also told me that there was a bagman's union with its own coat of arms. 'There used to be a coat of arms that was drawn in a circle like a shield and it was divided in three. The swag at the bottom, the blackened billy can in the left hand corner and the ration card in the other corner. On most of the bridges and campsites you'd find it scratched in charcoal.' In *Australian Tradition* magazine (December 1970). Wendy Lowenstein added, 'The Bagman's Union had a self-appointed president named Kemp. There were no other office bearers, the head office being wherever the president happened to be camped. Kemp had a book of rules printed which stipulated the regulations for accepting tucker, lifts on the road, opening and shutting of gates, treatment of dogs, sharing fires, correct method of carrying bags and billycans. A member was allowed to have two straps on his swag, but after five years on the track he was entitled to add a third strap which elevated him to the rank of sergeant.'

———— • ————

In the swagman's estimation, the squatter's either a good cove or bad cove. The oldtimers used to say that just as the liver works the tucker bag rises or falls or the barometer of the belly regulates the stomach ethic. If the squatter gives him a pint of dust [flour], a banjo of mutton [shoulder] and a pinch of dynamite [baking powder], he goes down to the traveller's hut and proclaims in a loud voice to all and sundry as well as publishing it in the Bagman's Gazette that fact that the squatter is the whitest of men — a blessing to the world and one of nature's fairest ornaments. If on the contrary the squatter presents him to the douglas (the axe) or gives him only a poke of dust (half a pound of flour) he clears out in high dudgeon telling the trees (not the squatter) as he makes for his camp that the wool king is a cow and deep dyed ruffian.

Anon, attributed to 'The Rager' in the *Shearer* Magazine, 1905

In the old days the sundowner was pretty right to get the standard station handout, we used to call it the 8, 10, 2 and a half. Eight pounds of flour, ten of meat, two of sugar and half a pound of tea. Today you still get 8, 10, 2 and a half... Eight minutes to get off the property, ten yards' start on the dog, two reasons why you could be had up for trespassing and only half a chance to explain yourself!

Rules of the Swagman's Union

1 No member to be over 100 years of age.

2 Each member to pay one pannikin of flour entrance fee. Members who don't care about paying it will be admitted free.

3 No member to carry swags weighing over ten pounds.

4 Each member to possess three complete sets of tucker-bags, each set to consist of nine bags.

5 No member to pass any station, farm, boundary-rider's hut, camp or homestead without tapping and obtaining rations and handouts.

6 No member to allow himself to be bitten by a sheep. If a sheep bites a member he must immediately turn it into mutton.

7 Members who defame a good cook, or pay a fine when run in, shall be expelled by the union.

8 No member is allowed to solicit baking powder, tea, flour, sugar or tobacco from a fellow unionist.

9 Any member found without at least two sets of bags filled with tucker will be fined.

10 No member to look for or accept work of any description. Members found working will be expelled.

11 No member to walk more than five miles per day if rations can be found.

12 No member to tramp on a Sunday at any price.

A bagman called in at a Queensland homestead looking for a handout but the farmer had been caught before and had a strict policy of 'no work, no rations'. 'Yes,' he said, 'we can let you have some damper, but you'll have to use the axe.' 'Strike me blue, don't you worry about the axe, sir said the swaggie, laughing. 'I'm quite happy to soak the bread in my tea — that'll soften it!'

Wheatcakes

Boil the wheat with blackstrap molasses and treacle. 'It'll put hairs on your chest!'

Joe Watson, Caringbah, NSW, 1974

Tomato Relish

6 lb ripe tomatoes, 2 lb onions, 2 lb sugar, small handful of salt, ½ teaspoon cayenne, 3 tablespoons mustard, 2 tablespoons of plain flour, 3 tablespoons of curry

Cut tomatoes and sprinkle with salt then let stand overnight. Slice onions into a separate dish and sprinkle with salt and let them also stand overnight. When ready strain through a colander and put tomatoes and onions into a pan and barely cover with vinegar. Boil for 5 minutes. Mix flour, curry, cayenne and mustard with a little vinegar and add to tomatoes and onions and boil for one hour.

Mrs Betty Griffiths, Adelaide, SA

Here are some 'lean times' bush recipes.

• Recipe for Curing Wild Pig •

Always kill in cool weather to avoid flies. Thoroughly clean the meat and to every 1500 lbs of pork take 1¼ lbs of saltpetre, 4 quarts of fine salt with molasses sufficient to make into a paste. Rub this paste well into the flesh and let lie for twenty-eight days in a cool spot occasionally giving the meat a rubbing. Make a pickle strong enough to bear an egg and allow the meat to lie in it for another twenty one days. The pork is now ready to hang and smoke.

Australian Journal, 1890

• Lemon Syrup Dumplings •

½ lb S. R. flour or ½ lb plain flour, ½ teaspoon baking powder, ½ lb suet, water and a pinch of salt

Sift flour and salt. Shred the suet then rub it in the mix gently adding water until a stiff mix. Put on a floured board and knead slightly then roll out ½ inch thick and divide into six or eight pieces that can be easily rolled into dumpling balls.

The Lemon Syrup: *Put the following ingredients into a saucepan: 1 cup water, ½ cup of sugar, 2 tablespoons of golden syrup plus the grated rind and juice of a lemon. Add the dumplings and boil for 15 minutes.*

Mrs Betty Griffiths, Adelaide

Pickles and relishes were invaluable in boosting the flavour of meatless meals. Pickles, chokos and dumplings with tomato relish kept many a family from hunger.

• Griffiths Family Green Tomato Pickles •

6 lb green tomatoes, 2 lb brown onions, 1 lb green beans (if available), 1 lb sugar, 1 tablespoon cloves and 1 tablespoon of chillies, 1 tablespoon mustard, 2 tablespoons turmeric, 1 tablespoon curry powder, ½ teaspoon cayenne pepper, 4 tablespoons of plain flour, ½ cup salt & vinegar

Cut up the tomatoes and onions and add salt. Cover with water and let stand overnight. Put into a pan and bring to the boil. Strain through a colander and return to the pan, adding sugar, then cover with vinegar. Mix the flour, mustard, curry, cayenne, turmeric and a little cold vinegar to make a paste. Stir in mixture with the tomatoes, etc., adding chillies, cloves, and boil for ¾ hour to 1 hour.

Mrs Betty Griffiths, Adelaide, SA

Easy does it when you skin a rabbit for the picnic pot. Photographed at Bathurst in 1904, these eager lads seem to be very serious about the job, though no less interested than the swarms of flies waiting on their backs.

Rabbit was always a favourite dish of the Australian working class, especially as it was one of the cheapest meats. Rabbits were common in all Australian cities and prior to the myxomatosis scare of the 1950s, many families ate rabbit once a week stewed, baked, boiled or fried. I well remember the rabbit-os in 1950s Sydney, travelling our suburb with their horses and carts emblazoned with the words 'Country Fresh Rabbit'. They visited us every week and always sang out their 'Rabbit-O Fresh Rab-bits' as a 'come-all ye'. This call was soon followed by a yell from my Father to 'grab the shovel and sugar-bag' and to scoop up the valuable horse manure for the garden.

• Rabbit Pie •

Cut all the meat from the rabbit and mince it, then add one onion, one cup of green peas, one tablespoon of flour, pinch of salt and a little water or stock. Mix all together and place in a pie dish. Cover with pastry and bake for 1½ hours at about 200°C. Reduce heat after about half an hour to 150°C. Serve with roast pumpkin.

Ernie Solinder, Cabramatta

Rabbits hot, rabbits cold;
Rabbits young, rabbits old;
Rabbits fat, rabbits lean;
Rabbits dirty, rabbits clean;
Rabbits big, rabbits small;
Rabbits short, rabbits tall;
Rabbits black, rabbits white;
Rabbits for breakfast, rabbits
*   at night;*
Rabbits stewed, rabbits roast;
Rabbits on gravy, rabbits on
*   toast;*
Rabbits by the dozen, rabbits
*   by the score;*
Rabbits by the hundreds,
*   rabbits by the score;*
Rabbits tender, rabbits tough —
Lord, spare me from rabbits,
*   I've had enough!*

Mock Chicken Casserole

1 rabbit, 1 medium onion, bacon, chicken stock cube, chopped parsley, pinch of thyme, water and milk, salt and pepper

Joint the rabbit and dip pieces in flour then place in casserole dish, adding chopped onion and parsley. Salt and pepper to taste. Put two tablespoons of stock in a cup of hot water and pour over the rabbit, then pour in milk to just cover meat. Put lid on and cook for about two hours in an oven of 150-160 degrees or until tender (which often depends on the age of the rabbit!). Before serving, remove lid and cover contents of dish with rashers of bacon and allow to cook for further 15 minutes.

Mrs E. T. Roberts, Canterbury, NSW

Fruit trees grew well in Australia and there was a time when most Australian families had an orange, lemon, peach and plum tree in the back garden, with a choko and a passionfruit vine hanging over the fence.

———— • ————

We used to make our own jam during the Depression. The procedure was to cut open the plums, or whatever fruit you had, and remove the stone or seeds, spread the two halves face downward on a sheet of paper or finely meshed netting and allow the fruit to dry under the sunlight. Take them out in the sun again and the next day until they are sufficiently dried and then we'd boil them down with some sugar. We used to make jamjars out of old pint beer bottles by removing the narrow neck by tying a piece of stout fencing wire around it and then placing the bottle in a red-hot boiling bucket of water. When it was sufficiently hot the bottle was then plunged into cold water and the neck snapped off cleanly. The jamjars had no lids so we would cover them with brown paper and paste them down with our glue made of flour, starch and water.

Gresser family papers

Smith's Weekly offered two recipes from the lean times on the Murrumbidgee. The Murrumbidgee sandwich was a slice of bread dipped in cold tea and sprinkled with sugar, preferably brown sugar, while a 'Murrumbidgee oyster' consists of a raw egg with a little vinegar and pepper and salt.

The Great Depression of the early 1930s saw thousands of Australians 'on the wallaby'; the census of 1933 reported that more than 33,000 Australians were 'of no fixed abode' and that nearly half a million were living in homes made of cardboard, iron, hessian and other makeshift materials. Getting enough food stretched the creative cooking mind of the average Australian. Times were very tough and it seems that the city folk were worse off than the country people. At least the rural dwellers could nearly always get enough to eat, but in the big cities unemployment meant no food. In response the government and charitable organisations opened 'soup kitchens' where bread, soup and tea were available to the needy. The soup was a 'whatever

Despite the apparent hard times, there was nearly always a break for a cup of hot billy tea. The makeshift home seems to be made out of box-crate timber and hessian bags.

was available' variety, and many songs, some parodying popular tunes, arose out of the frustration this occasionally caused. Many returned soldiers from World War I felt they had been betrayed, and understandably many songs such as the following were widely circulated.

• S o u p , S o u p , S o u p •
(Parody: My Bonnie Lies Over the Ocean)

We're spending our nights in the
doss-house,
We're spending our days on the street,
We're searching for work but we
find none,
We wish we had something to eat.

Chorus
Soup, soup, soup, soup
They gave us a big plate of loop-the-loop,

Soup, soup, soup, soup,
They gave us a big plate of soup.

We went out to fight for our country,
We went out to bleed and to die,
We thought that our country would
help us,
But this was our country's reply:

Soup, soup, soup, soup, etc

Another parody, to the tune of 'It's a Long Way to Tipperary,' commented:

It's a long way down the soup-line,
It's a long way to go.
It's a long way down the soup-line,
And the soup is thin I know.

Goodbye, good old pork chops,
Farewell, beefsteak rare;
It's a long way down the soup-line,
But my soup is there!

Swagman Jack Pobar, 1973

At first when unemployment got bad they didn't give coupons. You all had to go up to No. 7 wharf — didn't matter where you lived — you'd usually have to walk in. It was five miles from where we lived. You took a sugar bag, and you lined up — there'd be thousands there — and you'd get a ticket. You'd have to take that up to the Benevolent Society rooms in Keys Street. Up near Central Station, it's about two miles from the wharf so you had to walk up. Depending on the size of your family you'd get food handed out to you. A tin of plum jam, a tin of condensed milk, a tin of syrup, three or four loaves of bread and a big hunk of meat cut just any way. That had to feed you and your family. There was no cheese or butter or eggs, nothing nourishing. No vegetables. And you'd be walking from the Quay to Central, and then stand in queues, and then walk home again, maybe for miles. It would take all day!

Ina Moran, Sydney, recorded by Wendy Lowenstein in her book *Weevils in the Flour*

The city markets were important for survival in Depression Australia. There one could find spoiled vegetables and fruit and bargain-priced near-rancid fish. The market gardeners, a large number of whom were Chinese, were sympathetic towards the hungry. They were known to leave piles of good vegetables in the back lanes of Paddy's Market in Sydney, knowing that the poor would soon find them.

Ever since the goldfields days, the Chinese had played an important role in our farming history and especially in market gardening. The pig-tailed Chinese vegetable man and his barrow or horse-drawn cart was a familiar part of bush marketing and by the turn of the century 'John the Chinaman', as he was nearly always known, was an equally familiar sight in the streets of our capital cities.

The Chinese market gardens were sources of food for many Depression-hungry families, many a young lad deservedly returned home with a bum full of saltpetre pellets after trying to raid the local Chinese gardens.

Depression Mutton Broth

Put two mutton shanks in a large saucepan and add three table-spoons of pearl barley. Cover with cold water and simmer for three hours. Peel and chop two onions, two carrots and a stick of celery, add to soup with a pinch of salt. When vegetables are cooked allow soup to cool and then remove fat (reserve for sandwich spread). When ready to reheat, add some chopped parsley.

Up the Sydney Road
(Pop Goes the Weasel)

Up and down the Sydney Road
In and out of the weasel
That's the way the money goes
Pop goes the weasel

Half a pound of bread and
cheese
A quarter pound of treacle
That's the way the money goes
Pop goes the weasel

Half a plate of mouldy rice
Half a steak and kidney
That's the way the money goes
Half livin' down in Sydney.

May Colley, Bathurst, 1973

Every night when I come home
Supper's on the table
That's the way the money goes
Pop goes the weasel

From Koop family memoirs (1870s),
recorded in Mt Gambier, SA, 1990

The poetry and traditional songs from the Depression, like the songs of wartime, are far removed from the idyllic and lyrical creations of the bush. They are full of anger and frustration and carry the sentiment: 'Why me?'. Many echoed the style of such sentimental Victorian tear-jerkers as 'Don't Sell My Mother's Picture in the Sale' and the infamous story of the 'Luggage Van Ahead'. This Depression poem is typical.

• The Haymarket Bootblack •

He was a Haymarket bootblack bold
And his years they numbered nine
Rough and unpolished was he, albeit
He constantly aimed to shine.

As proud as a king on his box he sat
Munching an apple red
While the boys of his set
Looked whistfully on
And 'Give us a bite' they said.

But the bootblack smiled a lordly smile
'No free bites here', he cried
Then the boys, they sadly walked away
Save one, who stood by his side.

'Bill, give us the core', he whispered low
The bootblack smiled once more
And a mischievous dimple grew in
  his cheek:
'There ain't going to be no core!'

An undated recitation from the Sydney *Tivoli Songster*
and composed by Chas Coghill

Potatoes were the staple diet of many families during the thirties. Not that they were that inexpensive, it was simply that they were filling and versatile. We called them 'murphies', 'taters', and 'spuds' and ate them every way imaginable: we had them boiled, mashed, baked, fried, chipped. We had them with pumpkin and we had them in pancakes. Mum even made bread with potatoes.

Peter Snow, Redfern, NSW, 1978

Chinese gardener with an obviously prized cauliflower, photographed at Bourke in 1930. This outback town on the Bogan River was once a rich area for citrus fruits and vegetable growing.

In 1934 this corner store in Riley Street in Sydney's Surry Hills was caught in a vicious price war when small retailers decided to undercut the price of van-delivered bread in order to keep the retail price down. An inquiry into bread pricing revealed that one-third of Sydney's bread was still mixed by hand, and that consumption in suburban homes had fallen from a loaf and a half to a loaf or less. There was a suggestion that the fall in consumption had something to do with the new fad of dieting among the female population.

• P o t a t o   B i s c u i t s •

Rub half a pound of cold potatoes through a sieve, and mix with one pound of flour and ¼ teaspoon of salt. Melt two ounces of butter, and use as much as is required to make a paste sufficiently stiff to roll out easily. Knead the paste well, and roll out an ⅛th of an inch thick. Cut into rounds with a tumbler, and bake on a greased tin in a moderate oven for about 15 minutes, or till a pale brown colour.

Mrs Goddard, Dulverton, SA

• S a v o u r y   P o t a t o   S w i m m e r s •

Peel three or four large potatoes, grate them into a basin of water, and leave for two hours. Then drain and mix with half the weight of flour, season with a large finely chopped onion, some sage leaves, or sweet chopped herbs, pepper and salt. Make into a stiff paste with water, and form balls about the size of a small apple. Roll in water and drop into a saucepan of boiling water. When they rise to the surface they are cooked. Serve with a thick gravy.

Mrs Knightly, Mt Gambier, SA

Chokos were another food I remember from the Depression days. They grew wild in many parts of Sydney and were a real nuisance but I always thought they were a real treat and would go out to collect them. Nobody in our house liked to peel them as they have a tough prickly skin and when you peel them they are quite slippery. We used to eat them steamed with a little butter and pepper.

Jack Mays, Lithgow, NSW, 1974

Eggs were very important. Nearly everyone in our neighbourhood had half a dozen chickens in the backyard. We'd get fresh eggs every day, at least when they were laying, and nearly always had two eggs for breakfast except when we needed some to swap for other food. We couldn't afford proper chicken feed so the birds would walk around the yard and even into the house. Every so often the axe would be pulled out of the shed and it was roast chook for Sunday lunch or a chicken stew that seemed to supply almost a week of evening meals, even if it got thinner and thinner as the week wore on.

In the lean times, families would compete to purchase the cheapest cuts of meat and then devise menus aimed at stretching the purchase as far as possible. Scrag-end of mutton was one such cut, and the following hints for getting the best value out of the scrag-end are typical.

Mock Crumpets

Mash some boiled potatoes until quite smooth, add a little salt, and press into rounds. Brush with a little milk, and dredge with flour. Prick with a fork to prevent bursting, and bake on a griddle. Eaten with butter or dripping they are equal to real crumpets and very nutritious.

Miss Bumblett, Koop family, Mt Gambier, SA

Milk Substitute

When there is no milk soak half a pound of medium oatmeal in a quart of cold water for twelve hours. Strain, and it is ready for use in tea, coffee and cooking.

Sara McCrea, Gawler, SA

This 1930s corner store was typical of the times. Who remembers when such stores offered a chair for their more long-winded customers?

• A Way with Mutton •

Simmer the mutton with an equal quantity of peeled and finely chopped vegetables, i.e., if you have three pounds of mutton use three pounds of chopped turnips, carrots, and onions. Any other vegetables can be used, but, of course, not greens. Simmer until the meat comes away from the bone then strain through a coarse cloth. Pick out all the bones and put all the meat and vegetables (which will most likely be a mushy gravy) into a bowl. Put weights on top and leave till the following day, when it can be turned out. This way of using the meat gives you: 1. A delicious shaped brawn that can be cut in slices and eaten cold. 2. A bowl of well-flavoured nourishing soup. 3. A fair amount of fat, which will be found on top of the soup when cold. If you do not care for soup put some sago in when cooking the meat and it will absorb all the liquid and fat. The sago will also help in making the brawn bigger and even more economical.

Koop family memoirs, Mt Gambier, SA

I was served with a notice of eviction and I was eventually evicted; and that five shillings a week (child endowment payments) supplied the rental for an unfurnished house... We lived on fried scones, mainly, because flour was the very cheapest method of producing foodstuff and... I was very proud of the fact that I had a wife who could supply a meal from nothing.

Mr Jack Mays, Lithgow, NSW 1973

Poetry flourished during the Depression; it was an inexpensive way to record thoughts and as the saying goes, thoughts are free! This poem provides cynical comment about the inadequate support given to those out of work by the government and the church.

I'm only an old relief worker, I haven't
got much of a life
I do six days' work every fortnight, to
keep the kids and the wife
We never have very much tucker, our
blankets are faded and old
It's weeks since the kids tasted butter,
we shiver all night with the cold.

M.P.s call every three years, they come
and solicit our vote,

They say if they go back to power, we'll
never be short of a note
The parson he calls when he's able, he
comes in a big sedan car,
Leaves a few quid on the table, hops in
and says 'ta-ta'.

He says we should grumble never, that
the Lord's looking down from on high
He says that it can't last forever, no!
someday we'll flamin' well die.

Herb Green, St Lucia, Brisbane, 1973

I went to the butcher and asked him for some meat on tick. He'd been giving some meat to this bloke for his greyhound dog, and he knocked me back. I used to get embarrassed, to have to ask for anything I wasn't paying for. People would share clothes, but not food very often. I borrowed an egg off a girlfriend one day, and we parted bad friends because I couldn't give it back to her. You had to beat it up and mix water in it. The milkman had already thinned the milk and we had to thin it again. You'd get a big tin of treacle and use that over your rolled oats. Eat bread and dripping, which is all right. You'd get sick and you'd just have to suffer it. Get fish heads from the market and make soup. We used to be hungry. We'd lie in bed and say, 'We'll get up and cook bacon and eggs!' And all the time we knew there was nothing to eat in the house!

Phyllis Acland, Sydney, recorded by Wendy Lowenstein in *Weevils in the Flour*

*With a wife and six half-
    starved kids, I tell you it
    isn't fun,
When the butcher comes round
    to collect his bill, with a dog
    and a double-barrelled gun.*

From the song 'The Bald-headed End of the Broom' collected from Herb Green, 1973

As economic conditions improved the Australian table returned to normal. Meat, dairy products and a full range of fruit and vegetables became common. As we approached the 1950s we ate corned beef with white sauce and parsley, roast lamb with gravy, three baked vegetables and a side dish of overboiled freshly peeled peas, beans or Brussels sprouts. Beef was stewed or roasted and served with a brown gravy that would have put a smile on any shearer's face, sausages or rissoles were served with pumpkin patties, fried fish served with chips, steak and kidney served with mashed potatoes, chicken (but only on special occasions) and rabbit. And of course, there were lamb chops, lamb kidneys, lamb fries, lamb brains, lamb and haricot bean stew, lamb tripes and lamb cutlets. Salads, not worthy of the name, consisted of weird combinations of iceberg lettuce, sliced tomato, sliced cucumber and tinned beetroot and pineapple rings — thankfully they were

One could almost believe that these women were in training as 'bread police': and what about Miss Hygiene in her lily-white uniform, but without gloves?

Something to celebrate!

FREE DOMAINE CHANDON BLANC NOIRS 90-3 IN YOUR FIRST CASE VALUED AT $24.95

Discount Vouchers worth $262.30

Chardonnay ONLY $6.99 a bottle

FREE:
6 Months' Membership

CELLARMASTERS
THE WINE CELLAR

Join The Wine of the Week™ Club
12 wines delivered every 12 weeks

WHITE/RED MIX: ONLY $89.40*
Valued at $122.20 *or* $29.80* per month x 3 months
Just $7.45 a bottle average ▪ **Save $36 on your first case**
1 BOTTLE EACH OF THE 12 WINES PICTURED

ALL WHITES MIX: ONLY $83.40*
Valued at $118.50 *or* $27.96* per month x 3 months
Just $6.99 a bottle average ▪ **Save $38 on your first case**
2 BOTTLES EACH OF THE 6 WHITES PICTURED

Then get a new dozen at the same price delivered every 3 months, automatically.

Offer valid subject to stock availability. Savings based on our previously published single-case prices.
Operated by Cellarmaster Wines Pty Ltd, ACN 076 727 949 Licence No. 50402618

or step up to the Special Occasions™ Series
the right wine for every occasion

WHITE/RED MIX: ONLY $119.88*
Valued at $159.69 *or* $39.96* per month x 3 months
Just $9.99 a bottle average ▪ **Save $39 on your first case**
1 BOTTLE EACH OF THE 12 WINES PICTURED

ALL WHITES MIX: ONLY $107.88*
Valued at $155.48 *or* $35.93* per month x 3 months
Just $8.99 a bottle average ▪ **Save $47 on your first case**
2 BOTTLES EACH OF THE 6 WHITES PICTURED

ALL REDS MIX: ONLY $131.88*
Valued at $163.90 *or* $43.96* per month x 3 months
Just $10.99 a bottle average ▪ **Save $32 on your first case**
2 BOTTLES EACH OF THE 6 REDS PICTURED

Then get a new dozen at the same price delivered every 3 months, automatically.

served only once or twice a week. For sweets we had trifle, home-baked cakes, rice puddings, baked bread and butter puddings and 'I love Aeroplane' jellies. We used all sorts of condiments, including 'Father's Favourite', 'Pick Me Up' sauce, PMG (which we would always call 'pig's meat and gravy'), White Crow tomato sauce, with the straightforward slogan: 'makes food taste better'. Rosella tomato sauce and chutneys of every kind including the ever-popular green tomato. At least the cuisine had a distinct Australian flavour and could never have been said to be a copy of any other country.

The 'back to normal' attitude soon turned to gloom as Australia became increasingly aware of the growing shadow of World War II. Food rationing began in Australia during 1942; a severe drought two years later made it more stringent than ever with each person being rationed to two ounces of tea, one pound of sugar, six ounces of butter and two and a quarter pounds of meat each week. Special rations were available for young children, pregnant women and the sick. Like the pioneers, we had learned to pull our belts in another notch.

'Are these apples Granny Smiths?'
'No, they're mine.'

4

A Little Crepe Paper Around the Jam Tin

This is the story of Gentleman Jim
Somebody threw a tomato at him
Now tomatoes are soft and have a thin skin
But that there tomato was wrapped in a tin!

Bob McInnes, Robertson, NSW, 1990

WE learned our etiquette the hard way — by trial and error. That great Australian humorist, Lennie Lower, hit the nail on the head when describing the Australian style of etiquette: 'The careful hostess will ensure that the jam is tastefully displayed. A little crepe paper around the tins will easily fix this.' Lower loved taking the mickey out of society, but he wasn't too far from the truth when he gave these instructions for serving up jam. Coloured crepe paper was widely used in Australia to brighten up a drab room, be it the kitchen or any other part of the house.

Lower had a few other classic suggestions to improve Australian etiquette in his newspaper columns.

When eating fruit, such as watermelon, the seeds should be removed from the mouth with the hand and placed in the pocket or handbag. At important functions it is best to swallow them, as it saves mucking about…

Many people are confused with the multiplicity of knives, forks and spoons set before them, and are inclined to make a haphazard selection, thus making goats of themselves. Remain calm and do the thing systematically. First of all, use up the spoons; secondly, go through the forks; then wind up on the knives. In the case of wine glasses and so forth, select the biggest and stick to it. I do this myself invariably and have never been tossed out of a dining-room yet…

At the conclusion of the dinner the hostess gives the signal to rise. I am not sure how this is done, but I think that a green flag waved two or three times is appropriate and at an informal affair just a cheery remark, 'Now come on! You've had enough,' would suffice…

Where the guest of honour is a man, he should take the hostess's arm when entering the dining-room. If the hostess is very far gone, another gentleman may take the other arm, a third gentleman going in front with the legs.

It is all very well for us to laugh at ourselves — and thankfully we do — but there is a great deal of Australian-made bluffing in the way we conduct ourselves socially. Australians have a reputation for being genuinely relaxed, even if a little awkward, but compared to the stuffiness of the British we are downright slack! Barry Humphries' brilliant character Bazza McKenzie, as played by Barry Crocker in the movie *The Adventures of Barry McKenzie*, caught this awkwardness down to the very last laugh. Humphries' other character, Sir Les Patterson, catches another embarrassing side of our attitude to the social graces. Personally I find all this humour too biting, too close to the bone.

In 1883 the People's Publishing Company of Melbourne published an extremely weighty book titled *Australian Etiquette or the Rules and Usages of the Best Society in the Australian Colonies*. The preface added that it was 'compiled expressly as a household treasure for Australian homes'. This noble publication laid down rules on a wide range of subjects, including who to invite to dinner parties, where to seat them, what and what not to serve them, how to avoid monopolising conversation, the dos and don'ts of picking teeth at the table and a staggering list of table rules. It is small wonder that Australians refined the art of the barbecue.

The book also explains that 'Dinner *à la Russe*' was 'all the go' in the 1880s: all the food being placed upon a side table, and servants doing all the carving and waiting. The style gives an opportunity for 'more profuse ornamentation of the table, which, as the meal progresses, does not become encumbered with partially empty dishes and platters'. Maybe this is where the extremely popular idea of smorgasbord originated, with its crowning glory of the dreaded beef stroganoff. At least it made the servants feel useful.

Penguins on parade. A formal business dinner at Sydney's Wentworth Hotel in 1958.

Obviously there was a great need for a book of Australian etiquette, for we did not have the tradition of polite European society. Our pioneers came from poor British stock, even poorer Irish families, government workers and would-be gold diggers. Most came from a background that could scarce put two potatoes together, let alone fancy cutlery.

As the population expanded restaurants were established, cities developed and society became more established. Entertaining friends presented quite a dilemma and many young women rushed to buy the 'rules' so they did not appear socially inept. One can imagine that there were some almighty blunders along the track. Australia's answer to Mrs Beeton's famous cookbook, published in 1861 was a cookbook published by a young woman named Flora Pell, who took it upon herself to lay down the rules 'Antipodean style'. It must have been hard work!

After the turn of the twentieth century, Australian homes began to change. Many kinds of home appliance were being made locally, and the use of gas and electricity was making the workload easier. The Victorian era had produced almost a glut of such products as silverware, crockery and cooking utensils, as well as new products for the pantry shelves. Mail order catalogues produced by the giant department stores were sent to every part of Australia as consumer goods became accessible to all. Next followed cookbooks, and we continue to explore the wonders of the kitchen. These

Afternoon tea at the Sydney Cricket Ground, 1934. The inevitable Thermos flask replaces the billy and everyone is being ever-so-genteel.

When I first looked at this photograph I assumed it showed a cookery class. However, closer inspection revealed that each cook was working on an individual dish so perhaps it is the kitchen of a restaurant or a large home. Such uniforms were common in Australia for domestic service.

were probably less important than women's magazines, especially the *Women's Weekly, Woman's Day* and *New Idea*, all of which carried recipes 'for all occasions' plus cookery contests, write-in segments, handy hints and cookery card systems 'for every home'.

Despite our historic bush roughness both society and class were highly regarded in Victorian Australia, and the so-called 'refined' ladies even developed cuisine and customs to distinguish themselves from the brash working class. At afternoon tea or lunch, for example, it was the done thing to always leave a portion of food on the plate; half a sandwich or a morsel of cake would make a suitable statement. In restaurants one could make a different kind of statement by avoiding the rissoles and sausages in favour of French dishes. One suspects that this statement is also made in today's restaurants where the diner is faced with a menu of Frenchified names and nary a rissole to be found!

Australians are generally relaxed about their dining and entertainment. This suits our outdoor lifestyle and our casual approach to home entertainment. We all love a stiff white table setting and grand service, but tend to be more comfortable with a few guests around the barbecue or even eating in the kitchen. (We have created our own style of etiquette and think nothing of handing a guest a 'tinny' without a glass — in fact a glass would be an insult.)

I took my girl to a dance one night,
it was a social hop,
We danced and danced and danced and
danced until the dance did stop,
I took her to a restaurant, the finest in
the land,
She said she wasn't hungry, but this is
what she ate:
A beefsteak raw, a lobster's claw, some
pickles and some toast,
Some tomato sauce with asparagus and
corn beef and some roast,
Some Irish stew, pig's trotters too, her
appetite was immense,
When she hollered for pie I thought I'd die
For I had but eighteen pence

She said she wasn't thirsty, but she was
an awful tank,
After eating all that food, this is what
she drank:
A whiskey sling, a glass of gin, she

made me shake with fear,
Some ginger pop with some rum on top,
and a bloody great glass of beer,
A gin cocktail, a pint of ale, she ought to
have had more sense,
When she hollered for more, I fell to the
floor
For I had but eighteen pence.

She took me to the family and said,
'We'd have a bit of fun'
So I gave the old man my eighteen pence
and this is what he done:
He broke me nose, he tore me clothes, he
hit me on the jaw,
He gave me the price of a pair of black
eyes and with me he wiped the floor,
He grabbed me where my pants hung
loose, and threw me over the fence,
Saying, 'Don't come courting my
daughter, mate
If you only have eighteen pence.'

A popular music hall song in Australia, this reconstructed version from Jack Brandon of Bondi
was recorded in 1975 and the complete version collected by Ron Edwards

Most young girls were introduced to society at a debutantes' ball. Nowadays they head for the disco.

• Boar Water •

It was out near White Cliffs beyond Wilcannia and the shearer had been travelling all night and was dog-tired when he finally arrived at the hotel for the 8 am breakfast. 'I'd like a couple of lamb chops please,' was his order. 'Sorry,' said the waitress, 'we haven't got any lamb, sir, but we do have some lovely pork chops.' 'Alright,' he said, 'I'll have the pork chops.' When it came 'round for the midday meal he came in and asked for 'a nice piece of roast beef please'. But the waitress replied, 'Sorry sir, no roast beef but we have some lovely roast pork.' Reluctantly he ate the roast pork. At tea time he sets down and orders 'A corned beef salad please miss' to which the waitress replied, 'I am sorry sir but we haven't any corned beef, however, we have got a lovely pickled pork salad'. 'Alright! A man's got to bloody eat I suppose!' After about two or three mouthfuls of the pickled pork, he found it very salty and asked the waitress for a glass of water. 'Certainly, sir'. After just one mouthful he spat it out exclaiming, 'this water is dreadful — what the hell is it?' The waitress hurried over and apologised saying, 'Oh sir, I should have told you that it was bore water'. 'Holy Dooley!' The shearer exclaimed, 'You buggers certainly don't waste any of the pig, do you!'

Dick Roughly, Bathurst, NSW, 1973

There are many stories, poems and songs about the bewildered bushman visiting the city to find himself socially inept and usually hot-footing it back to the relative safety of the bush. In reality the bushman did find the city overpowering, especially the restaurants, where so many 'unusual' dishes were on offering. For a man who had spent most of his life in the bush where he knew everyone in a three-hundred-mile radius, the big smoke was a nightmare: endless streets with endless traffic, far too much choice of everything plus the sheer excitement of being there. Small wonder that most of them ended up at the horse races and those hotels that cater for the bush visitor. Many of these 'country comfort' hotels even went as far as establishing menus that owed more to the bush counter lunch than the available produce of the city markets.

The stockman had earned a spree in town and found himself in Sydney staying at the Australia Hotel. Not being able to read or write he asked the waiter to 'Bring him something special, something nice to eat'. The waiter, an obliging chap, returned with a large plate of Sydney Harbour prawns on a bed of shredded lettuce leaves. After a while the bushie signalled to the waiter, 'Pierre, how much do I owe you for the tucker?' 'That will be one pound, sir'. As the waiter handed him the bill, he noticed that the prawns had all been pushed to the side of the plate, untouched. 'But sir, you didn't eat your meal, was there something wrong?' 'Well, the grass was just okay, but be blowed if I was going to eat the bloody grasshoppers!'

This is the story of Mulga Jim
And the terrible thing that happened
to him.
Down in town on his yearly jaunt
He wandered into a restaurant...
Time came to order his second course:
'Roast lamb, sir, or boiled with caper
sauce?'
'I reckon it's mainly good meat spoiled,
But blimey, I'll chance it — bring it
boiled!'
The dish was served — he sat and stared
With stoney eyes; at the capers glared.
He grabbed for his hat and upset his tea,

Then shouted, 'Missus, you can't fool
me —
In over twenty sheds I've shore
And lady, I've seen them things before.'
He broke for the station and boarded
the train
That took him back to the bush again.
As he tells this tale by the campfire's
blaze
He ends up with, 'Boys, spare me days!
Starve the lizards and strike me
brown —
They don't waste much of a sheep in
town!'

Although by the turn of the twentieth century many fine restaurants were available, the average city-dwelling family could not afford such a luxury and they contented themselves with boat rides around the harbour and *al fresco* meals supplied by the likes of the fried fish man and the saveloy sellers. In Sydney the opportunity for a ferry ride followed by hot fish and chips was a real treat and every Sunday would see thousands of beach-bound picnickers with their steaming fish and chips wrapped in newspaper.

This song about the fried fish man is interesting as the composer includes street cries and a little poetic licence that allows snow on the city footpaths.

Saveloy
(Tune: Hold Your Hand out, Naughty Boy)

One evening at the hotel tea
and toast
I was there. I declare.
I went to have some supper with
the host,
So I ordered up a penny saveloy
And when they brought it up it
looked a treat
Full of meat, nice and sweet
When I put that thing away
There was something seemed
to say
You'll be sorry, let us pray,
saveloy.

Saveloy, I thought I saw you
breathing
Saveloy, your skin you'll soon
be leaving
When you are lying on that
coffee stall
Saveloy, you naughty boy
Last night I saw you walking
In my sleep I heard you talking
Saveloy, ship ahoy, you're a
naughty
Nasty, dirty little saveloy.

Written by Fred Bluett and printed in the *Imperial Songster* 1909

Ev'ry evening when I wander home,
I can hear somebody cry
Seems to be about a mile away
And then it seems to be close by
That's funny old Bill, the fried fish man,
Who keeps the fried fish stall
When Bill's about — don't he shout
His old familiar cry:

Chorus
Hello! Here he comes along the street,
A-singing 'Fried fish! Taters!'
Shouting out to everyone he'll meet,
'All hot from the old pie-can!'

Every now and then you'll hear
him yell:
'Hot rolls — a sav-a-deloy!'
Oh, come and buy, won't you try
And patronise the fried fish man!

In the winter when your nose turns red,
And the snow lies on the ground
See Bill a coming with his old tin can,
He's off on his round,
Shouting out: 'A fried fish-a-fish all hot
So taste before you buy.'
And wet or fine, rain or shine,
You hear the same old cry.

Written by Alan Rattray and published in the *Imperial Songster No 85* about 1908, with a notation that it was sung with tremendous success by Miss Vera Ferrance and Frank Yorke

———— • ————

Saveloys were extremely popular in colonial Australia, and they continue to be so! Nowadays they tend to be of dubious contents and the colouring is a very vivid red. They seem to be part and parcel of our sports culture and obviously need a beer to flush them down. The saveloys of yesterday reputedly tasted much better, even if we did refer to them as 'gasbags'.

Looking back we can see how much we have changed and how food fads have come and gone. Remember the fondue dinner parties where Australians tortured their palates with miniature pitchforks? What about all those designer layered sandwiches, and asparagus in curled bread?

• The Saveloy Man •

In Paddy's Market a long time ago,
There lived an old maid in the life of woe,
She was past forty-five and had a face
   like tan,
When she fell in love with the saveloy man.

How much she admired the saveloy man
For he was such a good-looking saveloy man,
That the lilies and roses to fade began
When she fell in love with the saveloy man.

Chorus
Yankee doodle, doodle dand
He turned right 'round to the bottom of
   the grand
Hot beans, pudding and pumpkin pie
The black cat kicked out the white cat's eye.

The saveloy man he began to dote
For his customers they owed him a ten-
   pound note
And of course, she replied, 'twas a scran
To cheat such a good-looking saveloy man.

'I'd marry you tomorrow,' said the
   saveloy man
And, of course, she well admired his plan
And she lent ten pounds to the saveloy man
For the old maid had fallen for the
   saveloy man.

Now he took the money and he went away
And she waited for him near all the
   next day
But he didn't come back and she began
For to think she'd been had by the
   saveloy man.

She went out to look for the saveloy man
But she couldn't find the saveloy man
And somebody gave her for to understand
He had a wife and seven little bits of
   saveloy man.

From the *Tivoli Songster* 1907, and sung by Johnny
Gardiner and Harry Sadler

And whatever happened to the home baking of biscuits and cakes? Up to the mid-1960s, almost everybody's Mum baked cakes and biscuits, and store-bought biscuits were a real treat. Baking was done on a Saturday and family members were often recruited to help in the mixing and pouring, and especially the washing up. There were real joys to be had by joining in, not

This is definitely a cooking school; the East Sydney Technical College catering school, 1950. I thought the girls were preparing snails but judging by the parsley and the whipped filling I suspect this is some type of 1950s savoury snack.

A silver-service afternoon tea in 1930. Note the silver biscuit server and the hot water pouring unit. Morning and afternoon tea became a ritual in Australia as we continued to emulate British traditions.

Anzac Biscuits

125 g butter, 1 cup shredded coconut, ¾ cup of flour, 1 tablespoon of golden syrup, 1 teaspoon soda, 1 cup of oats, pinch of salt, ¾ cup sugar

Melt the butter and add the syrup and then add the soda which should be dissolved in two tablespoons of boiling water. Beat mixture for one minute and add other ingredients. Put mixture flat on a cold greased slide and bake till nice and brown. The biscuits should be crisp.

Mrs W. Henderson, Heathcote, NSW

Question: What's the hardest thing to do in an Australian kitchen?
Answer: Milk Arrowroot biscuits.

the least being the opportunity to take a giant spoonful of moist cake mix which always tasted heavenly. Cakes came in all shapes and sizes, and flavours including orange cake, marble or rainbow cake, sponge cake, caraway seed cake, poppy seed cake, chocolate cake and those little cup cakes that were ever so popular. We also bestowed fancy names like Vanilla Snow Cake, Angel Cake, Fairy Cake and Butterfly Cake. Icing was also part of the ritual and the creative cook gave free rein to her favourite flavourings and decorations. On Saturday afternoons, we mowed the lawn, washed the car and then sat down to afternoon tea and cake. Biscuits were also baked, the most famous being the Anzac biscuit.

Around the mid 1960s the American word 'cookie' came into our vernacular. (Maybe this had something to do with the popular television series *77 Sunset Strip*, which had a popular character called 'Cookie', played by Edd Byrnes.) I object to the Americanisation of our culinary terms, and the Australian commercial biscuit manufacturers have — thankfully — continued to market their biscuits as biscuits! The favourite Australian biscuits have always been the Sao, Ryvita, Milk Arrowroot, Jatz and Thin Captain, with the sweet biscuit line-up including Adora Cream Wafers, Fruit Pillows, Iced Vo-Vos and Chocolate Montes. The various states had their own biscuit manufacturers: New South Wales's Arnott's had to stand up against Victoria's Swallow's, and Weston's and Brockhoff's. The picturesque bright red Arnott's delivery vans, complete with their parrot emblem, are still a welcome sight on the roads of New South Wales. No doubt encouraged by the biscuit manufacturers, women's magazines featured creative ways of using commercial biscuits in the home. Sao biscuits, for example, could be turned into that famous classic the vanilla slice by slopping in some firm custard and adding a topping of pink or passionfruit icing.

Scones are also very much part of our food folklore; nearly every Australian cook has a family recipe to ensure that the scones are as good as Mum's were. (Of course, scones are nothing more than a fancy name for what bush cooks called brownies or Johnny cakes and the same general principle applies: a good scone should stick to your ribs.) You can still find Devonshire tea being offered in the country, which traditionally means fresh scones with butter, fruit jam, a great dollop of fresh whipped cream and, of course, a pot of tea. Nowadays we have microwaved scones almost instantly, butter and jam in tiny individual serves, cream that comes out of a can like fly spray and, of course, a pot of tea made with teabags. It just isn't the same as the following:

• Scottie Scones •

Using a sieve, mix the following dry ingredients: 2 cups of flour, pinch of salt, ½ teaspoon of baking soda and ½ teaspoon of cream of tartar. Rub lightly, mixing in a little milk, a dab of butter and a teaspoon of golden syrup. Roll all this mixture on a moist board and make a roll about ¾ inch thick then cut into triangular pieces. Bake on an electric fry-pan ('they used to use griddles') turning when they get crisp and brown.

Mrs R. Overton, Cressnock, NSW

Our family was keen on pikelets, and 'Sydney Flour was our flour'. Despite searching high and low I haven't been able to find the Australian origin of the pikelet but I do have a family recipe shown opposite.

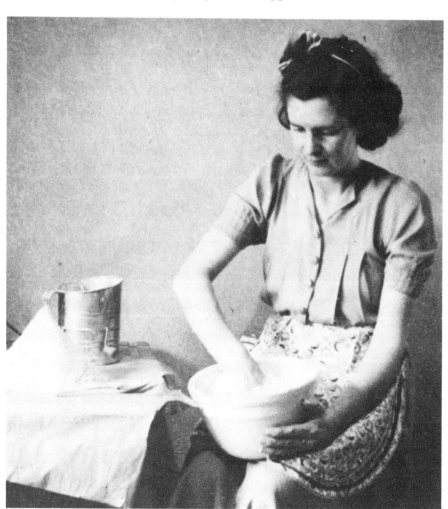

A Handful of Assorted Food Lore from the Australian Kitchen

- Put a piece of bread in your mouth as you peel onions and you won't cry. You can also peel them under the tap to avoid tears
- Spilled salt had to be thrown over the shoulder
- Carrots improve your eyesight
- An apple a day keeps the doctor away
- Fish is brain food
- Eating an apple will clean your teeth
- The chicken wishbone brings luck to the one who has the bigger part of the snapped bone
- The crust end of the bread loaf is called the heel
- Rice doesn't like to be looked at while cooking

Pikelets

1½ cups flour, 1 egg, 2 tablespoons sugar, 1 teaspoon golden syrup, ½ teaspoon baking powder, 2 tablespoons sugar, 4 tablespoons of water, 1 teaspoon cream of tartar, 1 small cup of milk, 1 tablespoon butter

Beat the egg and sugar till light and frothy, then add dry ingredients. Lastly add the melted butter in boiling water — hot water and butter is the Fahey secret ingredient for successful pikelets. Use a hot slightly greased griddle or pan and pour small pikelet drops with a spoon. Cook till nicely brown. Eat with jam.

You can forget those modern whizzamajigs; the only sure way to mix a cake is by hand. This photograph was taken at Rose Bay, NSW, in 1942.

Some Favourite Party Snacks

Cheese Straws Mix the following into a paste: 125 g flour, 150 g butter, 175 g grated cheddar cheese, ½ teaspoon cayenne pepper, ½ teaspoon salt and ½ teaspoon baking powder. Roll out three times, cut into pieces about half an inch wide and four inches long. Brush with a beaten egg and place in hot oven for about five minutes.

Mrs G. O'Malley, Five Dock, NSW

Savoury Dip ½ packet onion soup, 1 cup reduced cream, 2 tablespoons of tomato sauce, 1 tablespoon of vinegar and, if you like, some chopped chives. Mix all ingredients and chill.

Home entertainment in Australia can mean many things depending on the home! The average party food of a few years back would have included savouries such as Devils on Horseback with some cooked bacon on top, the inevitable Jatz biscuits with cheese, cabanossi pieces, prunes with an almond jammed into them, egg halves with mayonnaise topping, crustless white bread slices rolled around tinned asparagus spears, celery sticks with cream cheese filling, and more Jatz biscuits! Later came 'rabbit food' vegetable plates with a selection of julienne carrots, cucumber, celery, cauliflower and raw mushrooms, offered with dips of every conceivable colour and content. More affluent hosts might have served their boiled egg halves with red or black fish eggs, fresh prawns on their Jatz biscuits and cold chicken pieces. Hot savouries were meatballs, baby frankfurters and fish 'cocktail' pieces.

Today's host has a wide range of savoury foods to tantalise guests and for those who really prefer to 'get down and boogie' there are just as many 'party organisers' who will handle the catering from go to whoa. Nowadays one is just as likely to be served Indonesian food, Thai, Greek or Lebanese savouries: there is rarely a Jatz within cooee. For informal dinner parties of largish numbers, we have enthusiastically adopted the smorgasbord. Originally from Scandinavia, the smorgasbord is found all over Australia, complete with its northern name. However, we did Australianise it by replacing the pickles and dried fish with our own ideas of what should be a real smorgasbord — and that could be just about anything!

It is fascinating to discover how we develop folklore; many superstitions, customs and habits are associated with food both in Australia and elsewhere. Some are based on fact, whilst others are mere fiction.

A 1910 country refreshment room at Glen Innes, NSW. There's nothing like a crisp white tablecloth to add a touch of dignity.

Eggs have long occupied a leading role in the customs and beliefs of many nations, including our own. All over the world, eggs represent fertility and life; in religion they are symbolic of creation and resurrection. Every Australian would be familiar with Plutarch's controversial poser of 'which came first, the chicken or the egg?'

———— • ————

It is said that an excellent method of cooking eggs is to pour boiling water over the eggs and let them stand in the water for about fifteen minutes. This cooks them slowly and evenly to a jelly-like substance leaving the yolk harder than the white and making the egg taste much richer.

Australian Journal, March 1877

Eggs are eaten sunny-side up, scrambled, as omelettes, poached, boiled, coddled, fried and when eaten on toast they are 'chicken on a raft'. They say eating a boiled egg is an art and some people seem to make it a lifelong crusade. There is the 'cut it across the top school' the 'tap it all over with the spoon then peel it' method; there are those who dig into the egg with the spoon and those who use the egg carton as an egg holder. Soft-boiled eggs have always been seen as 'invalid food': any sort of upset stomach, sporting injury or cold called for a meal of soft-boiled eggs and Vegemite toast. Gastric conditions meant two hard-boiled eggs and a glass of milk of magnesia.

Every Australian schoolchild was once familiar with the radio joke 'No more curried eggs for you, sir!', repeated any time someone belched or farted (polite Australians tend to say 'Did you break wind'?). Kids also used to call a Chinese man 'Hoo Flung Dung' which, one suspects, is a derivative of Egg Foo Yung which seems to be a relative of the dubious Chop Suey.

This photograph was taken at the Crow's Nest markets in Sydney's North Shore and dates back to the 1950s when you could buy choice peaches at sixpence a pound and pumpkin cost threepence ha'penny.

Egg Flip

Put one well-beaten egg into a tumbler with half a teaspoon of sugar and a pinch of salt. Fill up with hot milk and drink.

Poor Man's Scramble

If you only have one egg you can still make a scrambled egg by adding a tablespoon of breadcrumbs and one tablespoon of milk.

Fluffy Ducks

If you like really fluffy scrambled eggs try adding a tablespoon of evaporated milk for every two eggs.

The Australian corner store was always a journey of discovery for a small child. So many jars, tins, bottles and sacks, with the smell of ice cream, fresh eggs, soap and biscuits.

Curried Scrambled Eggs

Melt some butter in a pan and add ½ teaspoon of mild curry, a pinch of salt, ¼ teaspoon of sugar, two beaten eggs and ½ cup of milk. Cook for a few minutes till thick and serve on toast.

Mrs S. Pester, Newcastle, NSW

Two swaggies were arguing around a campfire. They seemed to disagree about most things, and they started to talk about their dogs.

'That terrier is the best dog in Queensland — he's a top drover, he's good at snowdropping and he's no trouble at all,' said one.

'Well,' said the other, 'no dog is as smart as my kelpie. He once drove a mob of 2300 rum kegs from Bundaberg to Hobart and didn't lose one!' This dog talk went on for hours until the older swaggie started to get very hot under the collar — or he would have done if he'd had a collar. He squared the adversary in the eye and he said, 'Look here, buster, I'll prove that my kelpie is the smartest dog and I'll bet you five quid he will get my breakfast in the morning!'

The bet was accepted and both swaggies and both dogs dozed off. Next morning at sparrowfart the kelpie shot off like a Henderson spring and returned with a fresh billy of water from the creek. He grabbed a forked stick and roused the fire then shot off again. Ten minutes later he reappeared with a freshly laid hen's egg, a nice brown one, which he gently plonked into the boiling water. He sat staring at the billy and in exactly three minutes he grabbed the forked stick in his jaw and edged the billy off the heat so that the egg rolled onto the grass next to the swaggie. Well, next thing the kelpie does a triple somersault and lands on his two front paws and stays standing there with his behind pointed to the heavens.

'Strike me pink!' the amazed swaggie gasped and at the same time, thinking of his wager, screamed out, 'He's disqualified! Disqualified!'

'What!' called his owner. 'What d'yer mean disqualified?'

'The dog's disqualified on the grounds of insanity. Look at him, he's mad!'

'He's certainly not mad,' replied the smiling swaggie, 'he knows I ain't got an eggcup!'

• Bushman's Egg Cure for Bronchitis •

Pour the juice of six lemons into a basin with six whole raw eggs (in their shells) and let this mixture stand for three days, stirring twice a day. The eggs will now be soft, so beat well until the shells start to disappear. Put mixture through a coarse strainer and add 300 mls of O.P. rum, 300 g honey and 2 tablespoons of sugar. Put into bottles and cork after about an hour. Drink a hearty slurp three times a day and breathe easy!

Old manuscript

Pioneering families were not shy about trying emu eggs, either. Considering that one emu is equivalent in size to twelve normal hen's eggs, they must have made very big omelettes! Emu eggs can be boiled, but forget all that three-minute nonsense; the average emu egg takes a good thirty minutes and must be regularly turned to allow even cooking. The bushmen had various ways of checking to see that emu eggs were fresh, as they naturally keep for about ten months. If they are covered in fat or wax, they will keep for years. I am assured by old bushies that emu eggs are deliciously rich and considered a real delicacy.

There is a marvellous song written by Stan Wakefield called 'The Sparrow and the Emu's Egg' and it's a cautionary tale in the tradition of many older folk songs. A tiny sparrow boils up an emu's egg and is all ready to sup when he peers in and falls. The egg isn't cooked and he drowns. The moral of the song says 'If emu eggs you eat, be sure to boil them for a week'.

Around the turn of the century Australia, like the rest of the Western world, went home appliance-crazy. Newfangled machines such as the clothes wringer became wildly popular, and the modern woman had to have an oven and an icebox, later a refrigerator.

Keeping up with the Jones family became a national (and international) obsession, and a race that hasn't slowed over the years. It really is amazing

Some Egg Lore in Australia

● Don't play with egg shells or you'll get warts!

● To remove a birthmark from a baby you must rub an egg over the mark for nine days.

● If you dream of eggs you will have good luck, but if they are broken your luck will be bad.

● An egg with two yolks is called a 'double-yolker' and the person who gets it should make a wish.

● Don't throw away the eggshells before the cake is baked, otherwise the cake will fall.

● Brown eggs are healthier than white.

● Eating raw eggs will make you strong.

● Placing an eggshell in cooking meats will gather the excess oil.

● Intoxicated people are often referred to as being 'full as a goog' or 'as full as an egg'.

● A little vinegar in poached eggs will prevent them breaking up.

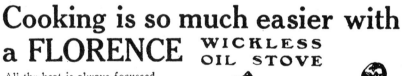

Cooking is so much easier with a FLORENCE WICKLESS OIL STOVE

All the heat is always focussed right on the bottom of the cooking vessel — no waste, speedier and easier cooking. Florence Stoves are clean—no wicks to trim, no smoke, no odor. Simple and safe in operation!

Florence North Queensland distributors, Messrs. Samuel Allen and Sons, Ltd., will demonstrate Florence Stoves in Townsville throughout the first week of July, at Charters Towers throughout the second week of July. See these demonstrations if you live in these districts.

BRANDTS LTD.

"Everything for Light and Heat."

236 Pitt Street, Sydney.

'Phones: M4651, MA1002.

Queensland Agents: J. T. Greenlees and Co., Ann St., Brisbane; Michelmore and Co., Mackay; Armstrong, Ledlie and Stillman, Cairns; Samuel Allen and Sons, Ltd., Townsville; H. J. Friend, Ltd., Gladstone.

Agencies open in other States.

Keeping up with the Joneses was never an easy task and this model kitchen of 1945 probably drove thousands crazy with desire. Such mod cons! An early extractor fan, an electric jug that simply plugged into the electric range, (very) centrally located sinks, a wall-concealed refrigerator and a tradesmen's hatch.

what now constitutes the modern kitchen: electric toasters, electric woks, electric knife sharpeners, electric Mixmasters, juicers, steamers, pressure cookers, toasted sandwich makers and, of course, the microwave oven. These are all considered time-saving appliances, but none is really necessary to produce food. As women are traditionally the home cooks, the appliance revolution has been part of the overall revolution to free women from household chores. No one can argue with the reasoning behind this, except to suggest that maintaining all these appliances must consume several hours that could have been used to prepare food in the good old non-electric 'hands on' method. Kitchen gadgets are something else, though: the vegetable peeler, the strainer, the sizzling steak platter, the corn twirler plug, the salad spinner, variations on the bottle and can opener, the bottle sealer, egg slicer, pea sheller, potato masher, cherry pitter, jar opener, onion chopper — and we must not forget the indispensable French butter curler and that Queensland invention, the pineapple eyer! For many years the hardware firm of Nock and Kirby's in Sydney employed a Cockney spruiker called Joe the Gadget Man who appeared in the store, on radio and television

Australia-wide. He was a 'gadget pusher' and his cheery sign-off 'bring your money with you' was known to every Australian.

Gadgets were vulnerable to fashion and subject to technological change. It is difficult to imagine a kitchen without aluminium foil, cling wrap or Teflon-coated cooking pans. The old bush cooks would have given their back teeth for such luxuries. Modern stoves also gave way to lighter cooking equipment, including stainless steel and aluminium, despite the fact that professional cooks still prefer to use heavier pots and pans, which tend to distribute the heat evenly. I must add that some of the best baked foods I have ever eaten have been cooked in the old-style 'Early Kooka' ovens.

It is interesting to see how communities react to technological change. When microwaves were first introduced there was a widespread belief that they would cause cancer and even blindness for those who stared into the light beam. There is still considerable suspicion aimed at the microwave, which we have expressed by creating what are now referred to as 'urban myths'. There are many microwave myths but the most common concerns the woman who tried to dry her cat in the microwave and the cat exploded.

Jan Harold Brunvand, an American Folklorist and specialist researcher into urban myths, comments, 'People's notions about what would happen to a living creature caught in a microwave oven are doubtless coloured by a vague fear of the new devices and intensified by such things as warning signs posted on public-access microwave ovens and the continuing flow of microwave-related urban myths.' I must admit that I certainly took some

The back-to-basics kitchen: be it ever so humble, there's no place like home. Mrs Donaghue comfortably seated in her kitchen in Wanaaring, NSW, 1905. Fringed paper was an extremely popular decoration.

convincing before I allowed a microwave into my home, and even now I feel a trifle worried if I find myself staring into the blasted thing. I once exploded a potato in it and all I could think of was the exploding cat story.

Etiquette is really a matter of 'horses for courses'; and what is considered good manners in Britain isn't necessarily good manners in Australia. Hollywood (or Hollyweird as it is locally known) has it that Chinese slobber when they eat, Arabs belch and Africans throw half-eaten bones over their shoulders. Maybe the customs of large Australian country pub dining-rooms could shock the gentle diner from the big smoke. Of course, etiquette is traditional rather than a firm set of rules and is therefore subject to change. Do gentlemen still stand when a lady joins or leaves the table? Do waiters still serve from the left, or do they seek the most convenient and safest entry? Is it now permissible to put the once-dreaded elbows on the table? One can even discuss the three taboos of sex, politics and religion at the table and, in fact, the dinner party that doesn't would now be considered dead boring! Times change and so do the 'dos' and 'don'ts' of etiquette, Australian style.

5

Swig, Guzzle and Swaller

The German likes his beer
The Pommy likes his half and half
Because it brings good cheer
The Scotsman likes his whisky
And the Irishman likes his hot
The Aussie has no national drink
So he drinks the bloody lot.

AUSTRALIANS have an international reputation for being hard drinkers. We are referred to as — and we call ourselves — booze artists, winos, groggers, piss artists, grog guzzlers, beer barons and bloody good drinkers. We go on the ran-tan, to a booze-up, to the boozer or to the rubbity-dub. We get shickered, full as a goog, full as ticks, pissed as a fart. We get home trying to avoid the booze bus and the blister and strife. Next day we recover with a stinker of a headache or a hangover, and the only way to recover is to have a hair of the dog that bit you.

In truth, we are not very sophisticated about our consumption of alcohol and it seems our rough-hewn reputation is well earned. Our Rum Rebellion heritage and bush shanty history might have played a role in creating our image, but many other factors have carried the early traditions into the present era. Our attitude to alcohol has always been one of social necessity wherever one or more men are gathered together, rather than as a pleasant addition to the mealtime table.

Australia's pioneering history played an important role in formulating our drinking traditions. Early Australia was very much a male-dominated society where the lack of female company was relieved by 'going on the spree'. Entertainment was also limited, so the pub became the focal point of bush society where a man who worked hard could play hard. It was considered his just reward!

Anyone who has experienced that thriving Australian country social tradition called the 'B & S' will know that the lines about 'sleeping on verandahs' could also include front lawns, street corners and the backs of pick-up trucks. The morning after a bachelor and spinster ball is not a pretty sight as the main aim of the participants seems to be to get as sozzled as possible and become total 'writeoffs'.

When people really get in the clutch of the 'demon drink' they are sometimes referred to being 'in love with the bottle'. That would probably explain the sentiments contained in the next rhyme which has been collected in several variants but with the same result.

In a young country, where entertainment was very much a case of 'what you made it', alcohol played an important role as a social catalyst and as a release mechanism for what many found to be the frustration of isolation. Poets and lesser beings romanticised about alcohol, providing drink with

The Truth is in My Song So Clear

When the sheds are all cut out,
They get their bit of paper;
To the nearest pub they run;
They cut a dashing caper.
They call for liquor plenty
And they're happy while they're drinking,
But where to go when the money's done
It's little they are thinking.

Sick and sore next morning,
They are when they awaken.
To have a drink, of course they must
To keep their nerves from shaking.
They call for one, they call for two
In a way that's rather funny.
'Now this won't do'
The landlord says,
You blokes have got no money!'

They're sleeping on verandahs
And they're lounging on the sofas;
And to finish off their spree
They're ordered off as loafers.
They've got no friends, their money's done,
And at their disappearing,
They give three cheers for the river bends
And jog along till shearing.

Traditional verses from the singing of Mr Joe Cashmere and printed in *Old Bush Songs* by Douglas Stewart and Nancy Keesing

• I'm Only a Lonely Bottle of Beer •

*He called for me when going home, just
   on the tick of eight,
Then walked along in silent thought,
   perhaps to seal my fate
He held me firmly on his arm though
   I was damp and cold,
He held me like a lover dear and would
   not release his hold,
Then he took me down a real dark lane
   where we could not be seen,
Then he took the wrap right off me,
   I could not call or scream,*

*'I've loved you all these years', he said,
   'although you're a curse to me,
If I could ease my love for you —
   a godsend it would be.'
He pulled the cap right off my head and
   lifted me up high,
Then sealed his lips right over mine
   and sucked and sucked me dry
Today as people pass down this street
   they see me lying here
An empty bottle thrown away —
   that once was full of beer.*

From Swagman Jack Pobar, Toowoomba, Qld, 1973

A drawing by S.T. Gill dated 1873 showing the 'boozer's club' in full swing complete with orator, toast-making, singing, sleeping and sundowners — even a swagman's dog gets into the picture.

various personifications. To many it was a fact of life, one of the rewards of hard work, even though most station owners wisely banned it from their stations. The songs, stories and poems of Henry Lawson are full of references to alcohol, probably reflecting Lawson's own lifelong battle with the bottle. His classic song 'The Shearer's Dream', for example, has female rouseabouts: 'every hour those girls waltzed in with whiskey and beer on trays'. Many other songs that grew out of the Australian experience had drink as a popular theme. Old borrowed songs such as the seafaring 'Across the Western Oceans' became a drinker's anthem as 'Across the Western Plains' with a plaintive chorus that ran: 'It's all for me grog, me jolly, jolly grog, all for me beer and tobacco'. Australianised also were chorus songs such as 'Charlie Mopps', 'When Jones' Ale was New' and 'Seven Nights Drunk' which became the Australian 'Shickered as I Could Be'. We also wrote many of our own songs, such as 'Lazy Harry's, 'Billy Brink' who 'drank sulphuric acid with never a wink' and 'Jog Along Till Shearing'.

The place was built of hessian
It wasn't bad at all
The menu it was written
In charcoal on the wall
The serviettes were chaff bags
The table was of bark
And you often ate a beetle
Or a lizard in the dark
And very often in the soup
There'd be an old bush mouse
But they always bulked their
* crushings*
In lousy's eating house

Ditty from the 1890s, Australian Folklore
Unit files. 'Crushings' is a drink made
from fruit and port wine

Unlike the British and Irish folk traditions there are few Australian songs about the actual joys of drinking in the style of 'The Jug of Punch' or 'Good Ale, Thou Art my Darling'. Most songs tell of being 'lambed down', 'dead drunk' or 'the day after'. It seems the closest we go to actually praising the beverage is the group of songs that tell of the anticipation of actually getting on the booze.

We also experimented to devise our own drink recipes. Opposite is an authentic, if not lethal, recipe for Bayan Rum.

Another special recipe was for a Diamantina cocktail, which consisted of Bundaberg rum, condensed milk and a raw emu's egg. A Mosquito Net contains a bottle of O.P. rum mixed with a dash of swamp-water (hence the mosquitoes). Delicious! It's small wonder that the bushmen had a reputation for 'earning their money like horses and spending it like asses'.

The old bush wayside shanties must have been rum sights. They were made of wattle and daub with rough-hewn timber, had a basic bar and tables, and served dubious drinks to wash away the dust. As they grew more successful, they would add 'improvements', but few of these early hotels would have looked like those portrayed in American Wild West movies. Large commercial centres such as Forbes, Bathurst, Ballarat and Bendigo would have had flash hotels, complete with brothels and stage shows, but these were exceptions. Later the shanties were replaced by the country hotels that we now recognise complete with verandah, dining room and accommodation. Many of these grand old hotels have fortunately been saved from the wreckers, but every time I go bush I see yet another instance of vandalistic modernisation as the iron lacework is dismantled, the pub signs and mirrors sold off and the basic character of the hotel replaced with 'phony coloney'.

Bayan Rum

2 gallons of overproof rum, 1 lb salt (to keep you thirsty?), 2 tablespoons of water, some leaves from a stinging tree, 1 lb plug tobacco

Mix and allow to settle for a couple of minutes before drinking.

Collected by the Australian Folklore Unit,
Toowoomba, Qld, 1973

I remember working out on a station in western Queensland. The boss had told me to drive into town to collect the cook who had been on a three-day bender. I eventually found Cookie and headed out of town for the station. We were halfway there when we crossed a dried-up river bed that had been in flood some months earlier. The cook woke from his stupor to see the bones of a cow that the flood had caught up a gumtree. 'Struth!' cried the cook, 'those bastards can certainly jump when they want to!'

Rad Dawson, Forrester's Beach, NSW, 1973

Many the bush worker who had been given his season's cheque made it only to the nearest wayside shanty. He might have had good intentions of travelling down to the city to invest the money in real estate or a small business, but the lure of the booze often proved too strong. It was common for the bushmen to hand over the well earned cheque to the landlord of the pub, only to discover that four days later they had drunk their way through most of the money including 'drinks all around the bar'. Certain landlords and landladies were known for 'lambing down' the workers by extracting as much money out of them as possible in the shortest possible time. The great Australian bushman and poet, Duke Tritton, penned a classic tale of lambing down that is full of glorious Australianisms and old-time words like strife, coot, decent grub, trimmer, mug, ugly brute, crook, swig and 'cornered like a possum in a log'. Duke called his song 'The Gooseneck Spurs'.

• The Gooseneck Spurs •

*I've been in lots of trouble, I've been in
  tons of strife,
But the fix I was in at the shingle hut
  was the toughest of my life.
I'd dumped a mob of weaners at a place
  called Leaning Gum,
I sang a ditty to my horse, 'Oh, Sydney,
  here I come'.*

*But I pulled up at the shingle hut, a
  little wayside pub;
Tired of mutton and damper, I'd like
  some decent grub.
The barmaid was a buxom lass, I
  thought her very nice —
You wouldn't think, to look at her, but
  her heart was made of ice.*

*I handed her my hard-earned cheque, it
  was over fifty quid.
There was a quick gleam in her eye, but
  her thoughts she quickly hid.
She smiles at me so sweetly and said,
  'It's getting late;
I cannot cash this cheque today, now
  would you care to wait?*

*'My husband won't be home tonight, so
  stay you really must.
I'd feel much safer with you here, for
  you're a man I trust.'
Then away went all my chances of
  seeing Sydney Town,
For that barmaid was a trimmer at
  lambing fellows down.*

*I had one drink, or maybe two, I'm sure
  it was no more,
And I came to in the dead house, feeling
  sick and sore.*

*It was the barmaid woke me with the
  foot of her little shoe.
'Get out,' she said, 'you drunken mug,
  three days is enough for you.'*

*A big bloke stood behind her, a nasty-
  looking brute;
I was too crook for brawling or I'd have
  jobbed the coot.
And the barmaid said, 'Your cheque's
  cut, you'd better make a shift;
Here's a bottle for the road, it is my
  parting gift.'*

*'All right,' I said, 'I'll get my horse,
  tonight I'll travel far.'
'Oh no!' she laughed, 'you can't do that,
  your horse has jumped the bar.'
And so he had. My saddle too; likewise
  my swag and dog.
No doubt she had me cornered like a
  possum up a log.*

*I wandered off into the scrub, I heard a
  dingo calling,
And soon I knew that I was lost and a
  heavy frost was falling.
I opened up the bottle and had a swig
  of rum,
It hit me like a hammer, my legs went
  weak and numb.*

*I knew I had been stung again, my head
  went round and round;
I thought I saw the barmaid before I hit
  the ground.
And I awoke 'neath a barbed-wire fence
  in a patch of Bathurst burrs,
With nothing to cover my freezing hide
  but a pair of gooseneck spurs.*

Written by Duke Tritton in 1905 and collected by John Meredith

The shearer's horse, dog and swag might have 'jumped the bar', but that was only one of the ways of lambing down. Clarrie Peters, a retired bullock driver, told me of one landlady who would get as much out of the shearer as possible and then give him a cheque for the balance. However, before she gave it to him, she would bake it in the oven so that by the time he had ridden to his next station the cheque would be nothing but dust. Another trick involved writing the cheque out with invisible ink that would eventually fade to nothing. Tritton also mentions waking up in the 'dead house', a sobering-up room supplied by certain hotels. These rooms, often without windows, offered a straw bed and nothing else.

Shanty owners also 'doctored' the drinks by adding tobacco juice to the beer, not to mention recycling the slops or adding water. Rum was also susceptible to additions that made the drinker highly intoxicated and sick. It was a common trick to give the gullible shearer a bottle of inferior booze for the track.

——— • ———

The old sundowner walked into the bar with a definite look of thirst on his dial, but it was soon apparent that he didn't have a brass razoo. He just stood there looking at the bar. A short time after, another swag-carrier appeared and he too was refused a drink on account of his poor financial status. It was a sad sight to see the two swaggies and their respective dogs just staring at the bar. 'Not a bad-looking dog you've got there,' I remarked to the first swaggie. 'I wouldn't take a thousand pounds for this dog,' he replied. 'And that's not a bad-looking dog you've got there,' I said to the second swaggie. 'I wouldn't take two thousand quid for that dog,' the second swaggie proudly added. 'What an amazing situation,' chipped in the barman. 'Here's two men with three thousand quids' worth of dog between them — and they can't get a bloody drink!'

Tom Haysen, Ulladulla, NSW, 1976

In today's hotel industry it is common to give drinks a name. Most of them are downright silly like Fluffy Duck, Leg Opener or outright American such as Manhattan or Colorado. However this custom is by no means new, and this list from the days of the gold rushes is equally odd.

Does a Bulldog Like a Chop?

Here's long life to Carlton,
Which I'll never hold so dear
If I get outside six glasses
Not the devil will I fear
Do I like a drop of lager,
Does a bulldog like a chop!
When I cease to take old lager,
Then the stars will surely drop.

As for Shamrock, dear old
  Shamrock,
Oh, the fun I've had with you
Never finer glass of nectar
Did a goddess ever brew

There's another one I'm fond of,
This Macracken's City Ale
For a drop of good City
Bet your boots I'll never fail

Castlemaine you next ask
  me sir
'Tis a drink that's fit for kings
I could drink it, sir, forever
But alas for other things
Want to know which I like
  best sir?
Why, I like the blooming lot!
When I give up drinking all,
  sir,
Have me, like a soldier, shot!

Melbourne song, 1903

• A Pub Crawl Menu •

A Stone Fence: Ginger beer and brandy

A Sensation: Half a glass of sherry

A Spider: Lemonade and brandy

A Constitutional: Gin and bitters

A Smash: Ice, brandy and water

A Catherine Hayes: Claret, sugar and orange

A Lola Montez: Tom Collins, ginger, lemon and hot water

A Hand of Hope: lemon syrup and water

A Madame Bishop: Port, sugar and nutmeg

A Julep: Brandy, sugar and peppermint

A Cocktail: Brandy, bitters and sugar

Files of Australian Folklore Unit with a note: from 1850s

The gentleman at the piano or the singer could be Charles Thatcher, as the venue is a sly grog tent on the Ballarat goldfields. Note how the piano is held open by a miner's pick.

That old popular folk song 'Lazy Harry's' mentions a dubious mixture of rum and raspberry: 'We ordered rum and raspberry and a shilling each cigar'. This drink was actually a bushman's favourite and had two nicknames: the Barmaid's Blush and the Maiden's Blush. It was also common to call drinks after popular personalities such as the above-mentioned Lola Montez. A 'Catherine Hayes' was named after a singer who toured the goldfields during the rushes of the 1860s.

Early records show that our colonial capital cities were wild places indeed, with extraordinary drinking bouts being commonplace. In 1844 a group of six bushmen went into an inn close to Melbourne and ordered the innkeeper to produce a bucket of rum and another of brandy which, after starting with a dozen of champagne, they began to drink. A few years earlier, in 1841, the population of Melbourne was 10,000 and during the year a staggering 20 per cent of the population was charged with intoxication. One suspects that this public show of drunkenness, be it in the bush or city, was

one of the few ways of relieving the tension created by the harsh conditions and emptiness of their lives.

One way of blocking out the despair was to hear the old songs. The old bushies loved to sing, preferably sentimental ballads or short and sweet ditties. Here's the parody of a well known World War I song, 'The Rose of No Man's Land'.

• The Nose on My Old Man •

Oh, it's the nose that grows
On my old man,
And it's wonderful to see,
Though it's stained with beers
It will live for years
In my garden of misery

For it's the one red nose the
*   boozer knows,*
It's the work of a barmaid's hand
Amid the drink and curse
There can be no worse
Than the nose of my old man!

Swagman Jack Pobar, Toowoomba, Qld, 1973

John Crampton keeps this inn
Where you'll get value for
*   your tin*
Rum or brandy, whiskey, gin,
Port or sherry, from the bin,
English ale (a perfect treasure)
or colonial at your pleasure,
Soda water, shandy gaff,
Lemonade or half and half
And last, and not least,
The finest dinners
That e'er delighted hungry
*   sinners.*

From the scrapbook of Charles Davies, Mitchell Library

The traditional song known as 'The Big Gun Shearer' is another classic bush story, where the 'green' bushie visits the city — in this case Sydney — and goes to a pub. The troubles never seem to stop. The anonymous poet has done a good job in capturing the scene of despair. There is almost a sigh of relief when the poor bloke escapes back to the familiarity of the outback.

• The Big Gun Shearer •

The big gun toiled, with his heart
*   and soul,*
Shearing sheep to make a roll
Out in the backblocks, far away,
Then off to Sydney for a holiday.

Down in the city he's a terrible swell,
Takes a taxi to the Kent Hotel,
The barmaid says, 'You do look ill,
It must have been rough tucker, Bill.'

In the city he looks a goat
With his Oxford bags and his see-
*   more coat,*
He spends his money like a fool, of course,
That he worked for like a flamin' horse.

He shouts for everyone round the place
And goes to Randwick for the big
*   horse race,*

He dopes himself with backache pills
And talks of high tallies and
*   tucker bills.*

He stands on the corner cadging fags,
His shirt tail showing through
*   his Oxford bags,*
He's pawned his beautiful see-
*   more coat,*
He's got no money — oh, what a goat!

He's got no tucker and he can't
*   get a booze,*
The soles have gone from his
*   snakeskin shoes,*
He camps on the bend in the
*   wind and the rain*
And waits for shearing to start again.

From *Bill Bowyang's Bush Recitations No. 5*, 1940

The Australian pub was, and still is, a magnet for yarn-tellers. However, the interference of television and the juke box is destroying this once-vital tradition.

The late Joe Watson was born in 1881 at Boorowa, in the southwest of New South Wales, and was a typical turn-of-the-century publican. He always said, 'I kept the hotel at Boorowa because it wouldn't keep me!' Another of his favourite lines related to the rivalry between Boorowa and the neighbouring township of Young. 'Boorowa was Boorowa when Young was a pup, and

I'm not sure what our Chinese friend intends doing with this crocodile displayed outside the Imperial Hotel in Geraldton, WA. By the look of the croc's mouth the poor thing is still alive.

Boorowa will be Boorowa when Young is buggered up!' As a country publican Joe saw the hotel as a social centre for the town. It was the 'home' of the local football team, the place one went to after a funeral, the place for celebration, a place for music and, of course, a place for yarn-telling.

This is really storytelling with a liberal dose of leg-pulling and joking; Australians have a real traditional skill at this and it seems to emerge with a few drinks in a bar. There are no firm rules and no real barriers. The same yarn can quite easily be repeated time after time and, in many cases, the storyteller changes the run of the yarn just as often and then comes around to the eventual conclusion. Certain yarners are regarded as 'master leg pullers' and are encouraged, by their immediate circle of regulars, to develop such skills. 'Tell us a story, Bill!' or, 'Tell us the one about . . .' are familiar calls in such groups.

The hotel counter lunch is well known for its good value. In the early days, many hotels originally provided them free in an attempt to encourage drinkers to stay at the bar. But they virtually disappeared by the turn of the last century, reappearing during the Depression of the 1930s when the concept of a meal for a small amount of money seemed a recipe for good business. Depression newspaper reports show that threepenny counter lunches offered boiled mutton, German sausage, pickles and bread and cheese. Sounds pretty good to me!

The names of many Australian hotels seem peculiar. In many cases, they were local nicknames that stuck. The local might have simply been called The Miners' Hotel, and that was that. Others took their names from remembered British names, such as the Three Roses, whilst still others went for the basic Terminal or Railway Hotel. Fortunately we weren't landed with too many completely British pub names, such as The Fox and Hounds or the Crown and Anchor.

Pub walls, being open spaces, attract local artwork, jokes, spoof signs and verse, which appear with the dart board and advertising. Many signs, like the songs, are anonymous. The most popular ones usually refer to credit or the refusal of it, and go along the lines of: 'Credit always given to those over 90 years of age, as long as they are accompanied by their fathers' or, 'I don't ask you for credit so don't ask me'.

• Why the Hell Do We Drink? •

We drink for joy and become miserable. We drink for sociability and become argumentative. We drink for sophistication and become obnoxious. We drink to help us sleep and awake exhausted. We drink for exhilaration and end up depressed. We drink to gain confidence and become afraid. We drink to make conversation flow and become incoherent. We drink to diminish our problems and see them multiply.

Hotel wall, Surry Hills, NSW, 1989, Australian Folklore Unit Collection

Joe Watson, who saw his hotel as a social centre where patrons could get 'a good drink, a good feed and a good song', told me that the very first song he heard on a phonograph machine was about beer.

Beer glorious beer
Beer, beer, glorious beer,
Fill yourself right up to here,
Drink 'till you're made of it,
Don't be afraid of it —
Glorious, glorious beer.

Joe also had another ditty he called a toast. However it is best known as a song:

Here's to the good old brandy, drink it down, drink it down
Here's to the good old brandy, drink it down, drink it down
Here's to the good old brandy, that makes you good and randy
Drink it down, drink it down, drink it down.

He added that 'whiskey makes you frisky', 'gin makes you sin' and 'beer fills you up to here'.

Australians have always been fiercely proud of and loyal to their beer, swearing black and blue that theirs is best and all others are undrinkable. Queenslanders drank Queensland-brewed Fourex brand, drinkers in the Hunter Valley area preferred their local dark-brewed 'Old' Tooths whilst neighbouring Novocastrians preferred Toohey's 'Old'. Sydney drinkers traditionally drank Toohey's or Resch's 'New', whilst Melburnians drank Carlton and Tasmanians drank Cascade 'because of the clean water'. Perthites said they would rather secede than lose their Swan or Emu beer. This loyalty has all changed since the late 1970s when Alan Bond and John Elliott became 'beer barons' and regional beer became national beer. The 1980s also saw the rise of 'boutique beer': small brewers promoted 'house beers' such as Hahn, Redback, Powers and Brewer's. Overseas beers also found a place in the large beer market; one can now buy beer from America, Germany, New Zealand and even Mexico. Loyal Australian beer drinkers like Henry Lawson and the actor John Meillon are probably falling down with laughter in that great pub in the sky! (Incidentally, it was Lawson who quipped, 'beer makes you feel the way you ought to feel without beer'.)

It's nice to take a glass
each night
Before you toddle home,
It's nice to take a glass
with friends,
Or take a glass alone,
I must explain my meaning
though
Before I let it pass
I mean just take the contents
And not the bloody glass!

— Common pub sign

Pub Table
(or How 2 Pints Equals
30 Days!)

2 pints	= 1 quart
1 quart	= 1 argument
1 argument	= 1 fight
1 fight	= 1 copper
1 copper	= 1 arrest
1 arrest	= 1 judge
1 judge	= 30 days

Traditional, found as a pub sign
in Bathurst, NSW

'Tis better to have a
bottle in front of you
than a frontal lobotamy.

Bob McInnes, Robertson 1992

Beer, Oh beer, I love thee;
In thee I place my trust:
I'd rather go to bed with hunger
Than to go to bed with thust
[thirst].

Anonymous

Clifton Gardens, Sydney, was a very popular ferry stop, and weekends would find thousands of work-weary Sydneysiders headed for the cool water and a picnic. These ladies seem to be having a jolly old time (1930).

Mineral water has also been hugely successful in Australia. Who would have ever thought that Australians would pay money to buy bottled water? But they do. A look around any supermarket shelf will discover at least a dozen imported and local mineral or spa waters including mineral water with flavouring.

The Australian barmaid is an important part of our drinking history. I have always thought it odd that hotels employed women to tend the bars in hotel saloon bars, but there they are right in the middle of 'no women allowed' territory. This 'no women' rule was a reality until the late 1960s when women began to break down all manner of doors, including those of the local pub. (I would wager that they are still not welcome in these bars, even though the barmaid is now more often likely to be a barman.) The Australian barmaid had to be tough; many a sharp-tongued woman has reduced a grown man to tears or stopped a punch-up with a glare. They were the mother confessors, too, and men would tell them things that they would never tell other women, especially their wives!

• The Barmaid's Dream •

*I am a young barmaid and my name
  it is Nell,
The young men of Sydney do know me
  quite well,
I'm fair and I'm handsome, so some
  people say,
And those are the 'mashers' who call
  every day.*

*One night in November ere going to bed,
I had some champagne and it went to
  my head,
Before the next morning I had a great
  dream,
And that's why I write this poetical theme.*

*I dreamt I was walking along at Coogee
And met a young fellow who accosted me;
He doffed his new hat saying, 'Hello
  sweet Nell,
You're looking quite charming, I know
  you so well.'*

*For a minute or more we had a
  quiet talk,
And then we decided to go for a walk;
We sat on a seat and he then said to me,
'My uncle's a planter and lives in Fiji.'*

*'So let's get a taxi and be married
  today.'
I freely consented and went right away,
I felt then as happy as happy could be
But now joy is over — there's none left
  for me.*

*At six the next morning I awoke with
  a start,
I looked for my husband, with a beating
  heart.
My husband had vanished and I found
  there instead —
A bottle of whiskey — lying with me in
  the bed!*

P. F. Collins Broadsheet printed by Sid Madden of Sydney and found
in the Lindsay Family Papers, 1892-1959

The look of the Australian pub also changed. The beer barons ripped off the old pub signs, replacing them with discount liquor signs, ripped off the user-friendly tiles that could be 'hosed down' and replaced them with carpet — yes, even on the walls! The counter lunch stands were replaced with buffets. The pianos were sold off and video machines were wheeled in. Dartboards were replaced by CD juke boxes and, according to many loyalists, worst of all — women were even encouraged to enter the public bar! Unfortunately all this upgrading has resulted in a sterile environment that doesn't encourage traditional entertainment like singing and yarn-telling.

The ambience of a drinking establishment is obviously important to the success of the premises, and the Australian hotel is no exception. The fact that most Australian hotels were owned by the major breweries meant that design decisions were usually made by executives; 'This year we will redecorate all our hotels. Let's take out the tiled floors and replace them with carpet. It will make the customers feel at home.' At least, one suspects that this is how our hotels were transformed into places that they were never meant to be. I lament the 'doing up and doing down' of our hotels, but probably it came about because of the desperate decision of brewers fighting to keep their clientele after the introduction of television in the 1950s.

Folklore applies to how we drink. The 'shout' system still operates very strongly in Australia where everyone is expected to pay for a round of drinks. John O'Grady's character, Nino Culotta in *They're a Weird Mob*, published in the early 1960s, provided many laughs in his first encounter with the 'shout'. We also call our beer glasses folk names. In Victoria drinks mostly order a 'glass' of beer but such a glass is unknown in New South Wales, where serious drinkers use a schooner. In Adelaide they have a 'butcher's glass', apparently so named after an incident in which an abattoir manager stormed into a neighbouring hotel and instructed the publican to only use

*Old Mother Hubbard
Went to the cupboard
To get a big drink of gin
When she got there
The cupboard was bare
And the old man was
  wiping his chin!*

Traditional ditty from Robyn Ridley

*Moses was the leader of the
  Israelitic flock
He used to get spa water, just by
  striking on a rock
One day from out the multitude
  there rose a mighty cheer
Instead of shining water there
  flowed Foster's lager beer!*

Traditional from Bob McInnes, Jamberoo
Mountain, NSW, 1990

Dinner at the Bega, NSW, Oddfellows Lodge. Waistcoats were certainly 'all the go' in 1939 and the same could be said for bottled beer. Notice one lonely wine bottle sitting on the main table, probably a port or sherry.

(Parody: Waltzing Matilda)

He lifts up his glass and he
drinks down his beer
And then he starts a yelling in
a voice that grates yer ear
'In all this bloody country,
wherever you may go
I'm the best, the best, the best,
The best at anything yer know
Best at playing cricket, best at
playing tennis,
When it comes to football, I'm
a bloody menace!
And I can cook a damper
standing on me head
I'm the best, the best, the best
Oh, enough said!

Bill Wannan, *Folklore of the Australian Pub*

---

small glasses at lunchtime — 'They are butcher's glasses!' He reputedly said, and they have been ever since. In New South Wales these small glasses were known as 'pony glasses', though the meaning has long since bolted. In the 1870s there was a popular tall glass of beer called the Bishop Barker after an extremely tall Sydney cleric.

The temperance movement was part of Australian life right up to its death knell, when the famed 'six o'clock swill' was abandoned in New South Wales and followed by Victoria in 1962. Early closing was supposed to save drinkers and it probably did have a reasonable effect, especially just after its introduction in 1916. The Bible-thumping wowsers stood outside 'notorious' hotels handing out leaflets, as well as singing teetotaller songs about families ruined by the demon drink like the infamous 'Don't sell no more drink to my Father'. On the other hand the 'swill' probably caused great damage to men's livers; hardened drinkers spent the final half hour trying to cram as much beer into their stomachs as humanly possible. It was estimated that 90 per cent of beer drunk in the 1920s was sold between five and six o'clock. In an attempt to speed up the beer consumption during the hectic swill hours the breweries introduced bottled beer, a move that caused great concern amongst the dedicated beer drinkers who vowed that the stuff never tasted like the real thing. Those were the halcyon days of the elbow drinker's art!

The painted hotel signs commissioned by the brewer Tooth's and Co. were well known throughout New South Wales and they are now a highly prized collectors' item. Tooth's started advertising their various beers on these hand-painted signs in the 1930s and for the next thirty-five years they commissioned nearly six thousand, featuring sun-drenched lifesavers, suave golfers, swashbuckling tennis players and rugged football heroes. The snappy message simply said 'refreshing!' or 'the ever popular dinner ale'. This was certainly one of the most successful advertising campaigns ever to link sport and alcohol. It is interesting to see that many of the painted signs were aimed at the 'sophisticated' drinker with paintings of glamorous couples in

the hotel dining rooms or in dinner suits at a concert or recital. In contrast they also produced signs aimed at the working man showing wharfies under a message that offered 'lager as you like it!' Curiously, these pub paintings were mainly restricted to New South Wales.

Brand loyalty apparently deteriorated at roughly the same time that hotel drinking declined — in the 1960s. It wasn't that we stopped drinking so much beer, it was more of a case of where we drank it. Hotels became unfashionable; almost overnight bottle shops appeared to cater for the millions of drinkers who preferred to have their beer in front of the television set. The hotel industry retaliated by bringing in interior designers and, worst of all, by bringing television into the hotel. Singalongs, dart boards and conversation were banished. Only the nicknames remain such as Whispers (he doesn't shout), U-boat (always sinking schooners), Crime (doesn't pay) and The Judge (just sits there).

Where are they now, the names? Federal Brewery, S & S Dinner Ale, Richmond Special Lager, Brisbane Bitter, Ballarat Double Stout, Federal's Non-intoxicating XYG Lager, Number One's Brewery Penguin Lager, Abbotsford Invalid Stout, Begg's Master Malt Stout, Alliance Temperance Ale, Perkin's Blue Seal Stout, Oakbank Beer and Sydney's Famous Toohey's Flag Ale?

One of the most successful songs ever to come out of the Australian experience would have to be the country song 'The Pub With No Beer' which topped our hit parades and even rattled up the British pop charts. It's a mournful story familiar to every drinking Australian who lives in dread that the beer will run out.

This photograph was taken in 1935 at a 'fake bar' at Sydney's Luna Park. Abbots Lager is no more, but most of the other brands have survived. One assumes these lads were under the drinking age of twenty-one, hence the joke.

(Parody: D'ye Ken John Peel)

D'ye ken how sherry and ginger agree
With a dash of rum 35 O.P.,
D'ye ken how it is when you mix all three?
That ye eyes they are weak in tha morning!

Files of the Australian Folklore Unit, said to have several verses

---

A SQUARE MEAL 6d

A REAL GOOD FEED 1/-

A PERFECT GORGE 1/6

1890 advertisement for a hotel
counter lunch

• The Pub with No Dike •

(Parody: The Pub With No Beer/Beautiful Dreamer)

I'll tell you a story, it happened to me,
A new pub had opened and the beer it
  flowed free,
I'd had several drinks and was full
  of mad talk,
Mother Nature came calling and I went
  for a walk.

There were blokes going out, there were
  blokes coming in,
And the racket they made was a hell
  of a din,
I spoke to a swaggie we all know as Ike,
And sadly he told me, 'The pub's got
  no dike!'

So I wandered out back in the chilly
  night air,
And saw about twenty more blokes
  out there,
Some yodelling, some cursing, but say
  what you like,
They wouldn't have been there if the
  pub had a dike.

Then I got quite a scare and my heart
  gave a thump,
I thought Bill the blacksmith was only
  a stump,
He got up and cursed me and said
  'Dirty dog!
Why don't you go elsewhere to run off
  your grog?'

'Twas then the top button broke off of
  me pants,
And they fell down and tripped me in
  a nest of green ants,
I yahooed and yakkied and boy, did
  I hike,
I couldn't care less if the pub had no dike.

I ran back inside over bottles and kegs,
My trousers like hobbles, still tripping
  my legs,
My mates poured some whiskey where
  my rump it was hot,
And the old spinster barmaid dropped
  dead on the spot.

Then a big drunken cowboy, eyes
  bulging like buns,
Said, 'I'll fix those ants, boy!' and drew
  both his guns,
The first shot he fired rang out through
  the night,
And the sting of the bullets hurt worse
  than the bites.

I got such a fright that I ran from
  the hall
And jumped on my pushbike, no
  trousers at all,
And vowed I'd make sure as I pedalled
  that bike,
That the next pub I go to really does
  have a dike!

Printed in *Singabout* Vol. 4 No. 2, published in 1961 by the Bush Music Club

And when I die
Don't bury me at all
Just pickle my bones
In alcohol
Put a bottle of booze
At my head and feet
And then I'll know
My bones will keep

Well known drinker's prayer

Australians might have always been considered 'champion beer drinkers' —
and to perpetuate this self-promoted myth we have written songs about the
amber fluid, poems, stories, film scripts and a whole breed of nationalistic
commercials that urge us to venerate the stuff. Popular songs like 'The Pub
With No Beer' and, more recently, 'I'm Going to Have a Beer with Duncan',
share the sentiments as 'I Feel Like a Tooheys', 'I Can Feel a Fourex Coming
On' and 'This Swan's Made for You'.

The past twenty-five years has been a remarkable change in our national
drinking habits. Many Australians now prefer to drink wine. Thankfully we
produce some excellent wines and, as with beer, we also create a folklore to
record this national interest and appreciation in the grape and our ever-
changing drinking habits.

The Australian style of toasting is typical of our rough and tumble tradition.
Some of them are old 'borrowed' toasts, some are lines from poetry or song
and some are pure doggerel. It is interesting to see that toasting is still alive
and, like children's lore, it is not unusual to find contemporary situations in
familiar packaging.

Here's to the girl dressed in black,
When you whistle she never
   turns back,
And if she turns back
She's such a treat,
She makes things stand,
That have no feet!

Here's to the girl on the hill,
She won't —
But her sister will.
Here's to her sister!

When I was young all my
   limbs were supple,
did I say all?
Well — all but one!
Now I'm old all my limbs
   are stiff,
Did I say all?
Well — all but one!

Here's to ya
And from ya
And to ya again,
When I met ya
I betcha
I wouldn't let ya
But now that I let ya
I betcha
I'd let ya
Again!

All above collected from Mrs Nancy
Cavanagh, Dover Heights, NSW, 1990

See that big white cloud up there
All white and frothy at the top
Just like a jug of beer.
It's time to have a drink, boys,
For if that cloud should burst
The beer would all run out
For it's just a cloud of thirst

Clarrie Peters, Austinmer, NSW, 1973

Here's a health to those that we love,
Here's a health to those that love us,
And a health to those who love them,
And we love those who love them that
   love us.

Swagman Jack Pobar, Toowoomba, Qld, 1973.
Mr Pobar added, 'There's a fair bit of hugging and
cuddling in that lot'!

Stringybark will light your fire
Greenhide will never fail you
Stringybark and greenhide are
The mainstay of Australia

Cyril Duncan, Hawthorne, Brisbane, 1973

Good, better, best;
Never let it rest,
Till your good is better,
And your better best.

John Furphy's advertising slogan
that appeared on all his water
carts and foundry goods

In the parlour there were three
She, the parlour lamp and he
Two is company
Without a doubt
And so the parlour lamp
   went out!

Elsie Elliott, 1986

Little dabs of powder
Little dabs of paint
Make an ugly woman
Just what she ain't!

I wish you health
I wish you wealth
I wish you gold in store
I wish you heaven when you
   die
What could I wish you more?

Charge your glasses high, lads,
And lift your voices high
For gold had been discovered —
One mile from Gundagai!

Quoted in 1956 Gundagai local history
publication *Gundagai — Its History,*
Verse and Song

*The sweet Australian wattle is the
emblem of our land
You can put it in a bottle or crush
it in your hand*

**Thump and shake the tomato
sauce bottle
None'll come and then a lot'll.**

*There's sixteen shearers standing
in a row
The whistle toots and away they go
With siding blows and second cuts
And half the buggers sewing up guts.*

*Me and me dog we travel the bush
In weather cold and hot,
Me and me dog we don't give a stuff
If we get any work or not.*

*Here's to the bull that roams in the wood
That does the heifer a great deal of good
If it wasn't for him and his great red rod
What would you do for beef, by God!*

Dick Wyoming, Forbes, NSW

*A little big of sugar and a little
bit of tea,
A little bit of flour you could
hardly see,
And without any meat between
you and me,
It's a bugger of a life, by Jesus!*

*We are we are we are
The Brocklebank Engineers
We can we can we can we can
Demolish forty beers*

**Here's to you as good as
you are
And here's to me as bad
as I am
And as good as you are
And as bad as I am
I'm as good as you are
As bad as I am**

**Here's to the man who loves
his wife,
And loves his wife alone,
For many a man loves another
man's wife
When he ought to be loving
his own.**

Imperial Songster, 1912

*Here's to the turkey when you're
hungry,
Champagne when you're dry,
A pretty girl when you need her,
And heaven when you die.*

Imperial Songster, 1912

**I've stuck to Queensland up and down
But as far as I can see
It's only when it's wringing wet
That Queensland sticks to me.**

*A rabbit has a shiny nose
I'll tell you why, my friend,
Because its little powder puff
Is at the other end!*

*Here's to the tree of life
Long may it stand.
It grows upon two rocks,
Upon the Isle of Man.
Here's to that little plant,
That doth around it twine,
It comes in flower every month
And bears fruit once in nine*

**May God above send down a dove
With wings as sharp as razors
And cut the flamin' mongrel's neck
Who tried to cut our wages**

*To the north, to the north!
The last place God made,
The contract unfinished,
Lost, stolen or strayed.*

**A wise old owl sat on an oak
The more he saw the less he spoke
The less he spoke the more he heard
Why can't we be like that wise old
bird?**

Mrs A. Blair, Balgoulah, NSW, 1974

*Friendship isn't just holding hands
And saying 'How do you do'
Friendship grips a fellow's heart
And warms him through and through.*

The tradition of a pre-wedding send-off survives. This photograph, taken at a buck's party in 1925 at Bellingen on the northern NSW coast, sees the blokes getting stuck into the booze. I assume the gent with the white armband is the groom.

I have no pain, dear Mother, now,
But oh, I am so dry.
Connect me to a brewery
And leave me there to die.

There's nothing Irish about you
Except your name in brogue

Rec. Lou Johnstone, Lithgow Donnybrook
Hotel, 1973

If your lips would keep from slips
Five things observe with care
Of whom you speak, to whom you
*   speak,*
And how and when and where.

Mrs A. Blair, Balgowlah, NSW, 1974

Not a penny off our pay
Not a minute on the day
Two quid on the pay
And a shorter working day.

There are many good reasons
*   for drinking —*
And one has just entered my head:
If a man doesn't drink when he's
*   living,*
How the hell can he drink when
*   he's dead!*

Don't wait to be told —
You need a Toohey's Old!

Advertising commercial popularly used in
Newcastle as a toast. Parody of 'Don't wait
to be told — you need Palmolive Gold'.

Here's to America the land of the push
Where a bird in the hand is worth two
**   in the bush**
Here's to Australia, my own native
**   land**
Where a push in the bush is worth two
**   in the hand**

Len Hattersley, 1982

The Wolgan boys are happy
The Wolgan boys are we
We never, never quarrel
And we never disagree
And the password of the Wolgan boys
Is, 'Come and have a drink with me'

Norm Muldoon, Lithgow Workers Club, New South
Wales, 1973; also Mr Arthur Russell, Maryborough,
Qld, 1973 who sang, 'The McGildy Boys are Happy'

Here's to it and it to it
May you ever get close to it
If you get close to it
And never do it
May you never get close to it —
Again!

Len Hattersley, 1982

Here's mud in your eye!

These two gals photographed at Kempsey, NSW in 1917, prove that beer-drinking is not exclusively a male delight.

• In the Shade of the Old Brewer-ee •
(Parody: The Shade of the Old Apple Tree)

The wind among the breeze was softly
winding
The brook was gently brooking to the break,
The village pubs at night were slowly closing
The row was like the end-up of a wake,
We stood beneath the brewery, you and
I, dear,
Your blushing nose you gently turned away,
I can't forget the way your breath was
barking dear
I can't forget it though, of course, I may

Chorus
In the shade of the old brewer-ee
With the beer in your eyes I could see,
When your dear voice I heard,
Like the old mutton-bird,
But it sounded like music to me,

I could hear the sweet buzz of your breath
As you said, 'I'll be drunk to my death'
With your skin-full of beer
I'll be waiting my (hic!) dear,
In the shade of the old brewer-ee.

In other pubs I've staggered since I
left you,
I've boozed in fourpenny bars far
far away,
And oft in thirsty moments do I wonder,
If you're as full as I am ev'ry day?
No more I'll see you lower away the
pewters,
The photo of the brewery still I keep,
And for the dear old spot I'm ever
longing,
So fill 'em up again my bo peep.

An obvious music hall parody, written by Louis Benzoni about 1906
and printed in the *Imperial Songster No. 72*

Few religions could match the rules, regulations and rituals of Australian drinking or, as it is sometimes called, the elbow bender's art. There are those first sacred words muttered after the first sip and sigh, the sacramental blessing of: 'It didn't even touch the bloody sides!' or 'Good to the last drop'. A beer offered without a respectable head of froth is considered sacrilegious and anyone who doesn't show reverence or at least respect for the shout system is out. The pub beer drinker is a zealot who will happily stand for hours knee-deep in cigarette butts and slopped beer to 'breast the bar' in order to get as 'tight as a kite' or 'full as a tick'. It is a near-mortal sin to count

the change scattered on the bar and even worse for the barmaid or barman to serve up a 'dead glass' — one that has not been properly rinsed and is therefore the reason that the froth does not cling to it in the proper manner. Dead glasses were a real problem after it became illegal to refill glasses in hotels. There was a great deal of opposition to this 'fresh glass', legislation as if drinkers suspected that a cardinal rule had been breached. Perhaps the worst possible sin would be to drink beer out of a straw. I have even heard it said that to do so dramatically increases the alcohol content.

It still seems only a few years back that Australia had those peculiar drinking shops known as wine bars where hardened boozers would drink glasses of sherry, muscat and port, but very little wine. They were scattered all over Australia and operated on a restrictive licence that only allowed wine-related drinks. I well remember the old one that stood opposite the law courts in Paddington, Sydney, and that later became an up-market wine bar called Martinz Bar and subsequently set the style for trendy wine bars right across the country. There is still a great deal of snobbery about wine drinking but the determined beer drinker can still bring them down to earth, as sozzled as he may be, by sneering at them as 'bloody plonkies!'

The wine companies of Australia have promoted their various products very successfully and, to their credit, they have set their own style rather than ape the American and European marketing campaigns. Australian names and images appear on our wine labels, the advertising is Australian

Wine drinking was always considered 'unAustralian' and 'arty farty' so the wine companies started orchestrating promotional campaigns to convince Australians that wine was an ideal accompaniment to meals. Many wine companies opened their own cellars where interested folk could taste various wines; some even opened full-scale restaurants. This photograph, from 1930, shows the Leo Buring Wine Cellar at the Ye Olde Crusty Tavern in Sydney.

BEER BEFORE WINE
ALWAYS FINE
WINE BEFORE BEER
ALWAYS FEAR

Traditional, collected 1990 from
Chris Kempster

A charming bevy of beverage maids. Look at the grape earrings and the daring short 1930s skirts apparently made out of frosted grapes and grape leaves.

without the flag-waving nationalistic jingoism of the beer advertisements and, of course, we invented the wine cask! One of our most notable wine campaigns would have to be the 'Where did I hide the Coolibah?'

One suspects that, apart from the old wine shops, the most damaging threat to our wine industry came in the 1960s when wine became the chosen alcohol of the so-called beatniks and then hippies. It was invariably flagon wine of dubious quality or, worse still, sweet wines such as muscat or sherry. Art gallery openings wouldn't have helped either and many the wine and cheese opening would have been more accurately described as 'paint stripper and soap cubes'.

The late Cyril Pearl, always fond of a good meal and a drop of wine, once found himself in a hotel dining room. When the waitress took his order he asked for some wine to go with the meal. The waitress returned with a bottle of sweet sherry. Politely, he explained that this was not quite what he had in mind and asked whether she could bring some red wine. She soon reappeared with a bottle aptly named Invalid Port and plonked it down on the table. Cyril pointed out that although it was a reddish colour, he was really looking for a dry red wine. At this stage the manager blustered into the room and eyeballed Cyril with a loud, 'Make up your bloody mind. This room's for eating and the bar's for drinking, so which one is it to be?'

Very few traditional songs refer to wine; overleaf is one.

• 'Ard Tack •

I'm a shearer, yes I am, and I've shorn
  'em sheep and lamb,
From the Wimmera to the Darling
  Downs and back,
And I've rung a shed or two when the
  fleece was tough as glue,
But I'll tell you where I struck the
  'ardest tack.

I was down round Yenda way, killin'
  time from day to day,
Till the big sheds started movin'
  further out;
When I struck a bloke by chance that I
  summed up in a glance
As a cocky from the vineyard round
  about.

Now it seems he picked me too; well, it
  wasn't hard to do,
'Cos I had some tongs a-hangin' at
  the hip.
'I've got a mob,' he said, 'a mob about
  two hundred head,
And I'd give a ten-pound note to have
  the clip.'

I says: 'Right — I'll take the stand,' it
  meant gettin' in my hand
And by nine o'clock we'd rounded up
  the mob
In a shed sunk in the ground, with wine
  casks all around.
And that was where I started on my job.

I goes easy for a bit while me hand was
  gettin' fit,
And by dinnertime I'd done some half
  a score,
With a cocky pickin' up, and handin'
  me a cup,
Of 'Pinkie' after every sheep I shore.

The cocky had to go away about the
  seventh day,
After showin' me the kind of casks
  to use;
Then I'd do the pickin' up, and
  manipulate the cup,
Strollin' round those wine casks, just
  to pick and choose.

Then I'd stagger to the pen, grab a sheep
  and start again,
With a noise between a hiccup and
  a sob,
And sometimes I'd fall asleep with me
  arms around a sheep,
Worn and weary from me over-arduous
  job.

And so, six weeks went by, until one
  day with a sigh,
I pushed the dear old cobbler through
  the door,
Gathered in the cocky's pay, then I
  staggered on me way,
From the hardest bloody shed I ever
  shore!

Recorded from Jack Davies, Leeton, NSW, and published in
John Lahey's *Great Australian Folksongs*

SPILLER, BOOSER & CO.

Anzac and London.

Agents in Gallipoli for all the Leading Brands of Wines and Spirits.

CHAMPAGNE
2290/- doz.

DRINK OUR WINES
YOU'LL NOT LIVE
—————— To Regret it. ——————

Shipments direct to all the Leading Beachcombers.

Our Genuine Old Imbros Whisky
(GUARANTEED RARE)
£12 per doz. botts.
NONE OTHER SEEN AT ANZAC. Ask the boys yourself—see what
they say—or the G.O.C.

Try our " Triumph " Brandy
ALL LANDING CHARGES SAVED.
Direct from Captain's Cabin Square 24 H 3, one mile from Kaba Tepe.
Or apply A.P.M., Anzac.

The Australian drinking style has changed dramatically. We now have 'international-style' hotels, drive-in bottle shops, motels, restaurants that serve alcohol but no meals, hotels that look like American theme parks and hotels that appeal to particular groups. And to add insult to injury, home brewing is also increasing! The fact of the matter is that our drinking traditions, like all other traditions and customs, are continually changing to mirror what is thought to be public taste. Personally, I think the hotel developers and breweries have lost the plot. Of course, such an evolutionary process should work in favour of the general population. But one suspects we have already lost control; who would really want carpet on the walls, crazy tile paths, Sky television, the CD juke box and television, all playing at the same time in the same bar-room? Did we really need a drive-in bottle shop? What about those nasty plastic orange garden seats?

Did we really want to see our pubs change so much? I suspect not.

6

Kidstuff

Andy Pandy, sugar and candy,
French, almond, raisin, rock.

IT is interesting to chart the taste buds of the average Australian child, to see how the diet matures with a mixture of common sense, flavour, experimentation and, of course, tradition.

We learn about food from our parents and teachers and this can sometimes create lifetime peculiarities. My father, for instance, would never eat pumpkin and always referred to it as 'pig food'. This might have had something to do with the fact that his father was 'bog Irish' and also referred to pumpkin as 'pig food'. I happen to enjoy pumpkin and so broke the chain — however, do not put a plate of offal in front of me as it can produce a violent reaction. I remember my poor mother had to always cook me up a separate steak and kidney stew without the kidney!

Today we have numerous scholarly books covering the dos and don'ts of diet, including several spelling out appropriate food for young children. Few of these books give the green light to cola, fried chicken or sweets, but kids love them, maybe because adults frown on them. The advertising industry aims campaign after campaign at small children buying media time in cartoon programs and there they are — the advertisers of all things naughty. Small wonder the kids prefer garbage when it is made to seem so important. However, they do retaliate and folklorists have already tracked several children's rhymes that 'have a go' at the purveyors of 'junk food'.

Certainly we learn from example and especially from other children in the family who cry out, 'I don't want that!' Hands up all those who were encouraged to eat by guilt! 'Eat it all up — there are children starving in India who would love to eat that!' (to which the automatic reply was, 'Name one!') or 'Eat it all up... it will put hairs on your chest!'

Much of our learning about food is by experimentation. I would love to know what certain foods tasted like on my first encounter — olives, garlic, pickled walnuts, gherkins, anchovy paste, chilli and so many others must have tasted, to use a popular children's expression, like yuk!

Children have always used food as an inspiration for rhyme and most of it is messy. How many Australian children squealed with delight in shocking their parents with rhymes like this obviously American favourite that found itself in the backblocks.

One potato, two potato, three
  potato, four,
Five potato, six potato, seven
  potato, more.

(Tune: Yankee Doodle Dandy)

Colonel Sanders came to town
Riding on a chicken.
Stuck his finger up its bum
And said 'It's finger lickin'.'

Schoolyard rhyme first recorded late 1970s

I must not throw upon the floor,
The crust I cannot eat,
For many a hungry little child,
Would think it quite a treat.

Rhyme in wide circulation around the turn of the century

*Two little sausages frying in
    the pan,
One went pop and the other
    went bang.*

*Ice cream and jelly, a punch
    in the belly,
Fruit and nuts, a punch in
    the guts.*

*Yum, yum, pig's bum,
Makes good chewing gum.*

*Great, green gobs of greasy gopher guts
Mutilated monkey meat
Dirty little birdies' feet.
Great, green gobs of greasy, grimy
    gopher guts
And I forgot my spoon!
But I got a straw!*

Rhymes about food have always gone with jokes: 'Mummy, Mummy' jokes, horror jokes and all those food-related elephant jokes. 'Why don't elephants drink martinis? Have you ever had an olive stuck up your nose?' Or: 'How do you know an elephant's been in your refrigerator? By the footprints in the peanut butter.'

When I was a kid, we weren't allowed to eat many store-bought sweets, 'They'll rot your teeth' was the usual reply to, 'Can I have . . .'. Our sweet-tooth fantasies were given over to biscuits which, in those days, you could buy as 'broken biscuits' served up in whopping big brown paper bags. The store biscuits were sold in bulk from large tins and it always seemed to me that more than their fair share were broken in transit. One shilling seemed to translate into a very assorted bag of Mr Arnott's best. In retrospect the corner store was a very important part of our life and in the days before supermarkets, we kids seemed destined to 'pop around to the corner store' every few hours to collect the bread 'And don't nibble the ends!' There was also the paper, washing powder and a zillion other things that always seemed to be in stock and within reach. We would search the Brighton Le

What young child hasn't mixed up the flour and sugar and discreetly popped the gooey mix into his or her mouth? These two charming little girls were photographed at Cootamundra, NSW, in 1911.

Sands beachfront in the hope of finding a refundable soft drink bottle for sixpence to add to our ever-diminishing pocket money. Our billycarts often sounded as if they belonged to Steptoe and Son.

Breakfast was always a hearty meal prior to the 'here's yet another diet' boom of the 1960s. We were a cereal family, a Weetbix family, our breakfasts consisting of two Weetbix, milk and sliced banana, toast, Vegemite and tea, or in my case, a glass of milk. In summer Dad and I would walk down to Botany Bay and have a swim in what was then clean water, chase up old Bingeye, the local trawler fisherman, and take home some fresh fish which we would eat lightly panfried for breakfast. It tasted like magic, but these days I would rather eat sand than fish out of Botany Bay.

Weekends usually heralded a more substantial breakfast of eggs and a slice of bacon each. I still can't believe how much food we kids could tuck away! In the 1950s cereals meant Weetbix, cornflakes, porridge, Rice Bubbles and, of course, All-bran. With television came a never-ending cavalcade of breakfast cereals: Coco Pops, Sugar Frosties, Weetflakes, Sultana Bran, Fruit Loops, and others. Muesli, that most sensible of breakfast cereals, was not readily available until the 1960s.

The popularity of early cereals had nothing to do with the nutritional value or the flavour but was directly related to what you could find inside the box — a toy soldier, a pass for Luna Park rides, a trading card.

Growing up in Ramsgate, a beachside suburb on the south side of Sydney (or 'steak and kidney' as it is also known in rhyming slang), I remember my

This is a very well stocked general store, probably in a large country town. Lots of familiar brands — All Bran, Bingo custard, Arnotts, Persil, Aspro, Rosella and Foster Clark's.

first encounter with salami. It was in the early 1950s and coincided with the first Maltese and Italian students who came to our primary school. There we were in the playground eating our sandwiches of devon, peanut butter, Vegemite, soggy tomato and cold lamb, and there they were with these whopping huge sandwiches stuffed with what looked like half a block of cheese and an equally large chunk of salami. Kids being adventurous eventually decided to swap sandwiches and one day I got my molars around one of these amazing sandwiches, and it was delicious. It was 'no more devon for me' and I never looked back. I doubt if the Zanollis and Zammitts were very impressed by our exchange sandwiches.

On Mondays there was no fresh bread so my Mother always gave me money to buy my lunch instead of making it for me. The school had a tuckshop (a word derived from tucker?) that offered sandwiches that hardly anyone bought, meat pieces, frankfurts that were never known as hot dogs, and rather strange hot concotions that included the Wimpy, an unappetising slop of overcooked frankfurt pieces in baked beans and a macaroni cheese dish that carried the unfortunate nickname 'the macapoo'. I can't remember the taste, but the smell was enough. There was also an impressive range of finger buns, scones and lamingtons that would do any Fatty Finn proud. Every day of the week we also mustered like cattle at 11 am for playlunch (what is the origin of this term?) and were made to drink a small bottle of milk. This might have been the government's idea of strengthening the nation's bone structure but I will never forget being forced to drink warm milk that we kids always called either 'moo juice' or 'cow's piss'. For gatherers of nostalgia — remember the coloured celebratory aluminium bottle tops on the Queen's birthday, Anzac Day and Easter?

Another feature of our school dining was the Oslo lunch. Now, this term sounds as if young Australians were destined to munch away at raw herring sandwiches. But it was named after a Norwegian doctor, Carl Schiotz, who developed it in 1932. The Oslo was first tested in Australia in 1940 at the Collingwood primary school, where fifty kids were randomly selected to lunch on a daily menu of three slices of wholemeal bread and butter with cheese, half a pint of milk, half an ounce of wheat hearts and an orange.

Apparently their general health improved dramatically and they gained almost twice as much weight as the rest of the school children, had fewer colds, their skin condition improved and they were chockfull of energy. Nutritionalists now realise that the majority of Australian children were at the time suffering from a vitamin B1 deficiency. The Oslo lunch was accepted and soon became a part of everyday school life.

A 1990 newspaper report said that many school canteens were caving in to student pressure to sell junk food, one of the main reasons being that there was an equally strong pressure for the canteen to make a profit. (In my days, students would have found it nigh impossible to exert any pressure on our school administration.) The article continued that the parent-controlled Parents' and Citizens' organisations were actually looking to ways of labelling the junk foods with more acceptable labels including, God forbid, 'traditional Australian fare' or 'treat food'. The National Heart Foundation found that most secondary schools promoted unhealthy foods when they should have been pushing fresh, healthy lunches and snacks. The NHF spokesman was quoted as saying, 'High-fat foods like potato chips, Mars bars and pies and sausage rolls were promoted and displayed prominently in most of the canteens surveyed' (Sydney *Telegraph Mirror*, November 1990).

Part of each year's school calendar was the annual fete and the Parents' and Citizens' Association encouraged all families to contribute. I know my Father contributed to the Esmerelda, the chocolate wheel and several other illegal gambling games. Mum baked cakes, made coconut ice (now that really *was* a sugar trip!), biscuits and toffee apples. Being a fete fanatic I can report

Coconut Ice Squares

Mix the following ingredients: 125 g butter, ½ cup sugar, 1 cup flour, 1 teaspoon baking powder and one egg. Press mixture into a baking tray and bake for twenty minutes. When cool top with the following mixture: boil ½ cup of milk, 2 small cups of sugar and 1 teaspoon of butter for about 4 minutes. When cool mix in ½ cup of coconut, vanilla essence and some cochineal to colour. Beat until fairly thick and easy to spread on base mixture.

Mrs Fotheringham, Sans Souci, NSW

Hedgehogs

Beat 250 g butter and 125 g sugar to a cream and add one egg then a sifted mixture of 1 teaspoon of baking powder, 1½ cups of flour, adding one tablespoon of chopped walnuts and one table-spoon of chopped cherries. Roll teaspoons of mixture in Kelloggs cornflakes and bake in a moderate oven.

Mrs Fotheringham, Sans Souci, NSW

Just about every Australian child was brought up gnawing a milk arrowroot biscuit and this toddler, photographed at Murringo, NSW in 1929, shows evidence that they built bonny babies.

MR. PEANUT

A travelling cafe photographed at Cobar, NSW in 1935. What excitement this jalopy must have created as it honked around the country offering ginger beer and confectionery.

that other Mums did the same and as I still find it difficult to pass a good fete I must report that the tradition of Australian fete food still thrives.

Peanuts have always been popular with children. There was only one favourite type of nut, the fresh-from-the-shell variety, and the Fahey family always had fresh peanuts on Friday night. Dad would bring them home after a few beers at the local pub and it was our job to handle the shelling. I well remember how fresh they smelled and tasted and how my hands would end up covered in the brown stain of the shell. Sometimes we would buy mixed nuts and spend hours trying to crack the hard macadamias and Chinese nuts.

While my youthful culinary skill was generally confined to washing up and drying, I was a mean hand with the jaffle iron. I don't mean those fancy electric toasted sandwich makers, but the real jaffle iron that still has no peer. One had to rub butter on to both inner sides of the iron then carefully place buttered bread on the iron and then the fillings. When closed the corner bits of bread had to be trimmed off and whacko! you were ready to cook. Seven minutes a side, and you had to be careful or the contents would try to escape. We jaffled everything imaginable but the perennial favourites were undoubtedly baked beans or spaghetti, eggs (very difficult!), banana, tuna and, of course, tomato and cheese. We used to cook them on the gas ring and tried to use the old cosy heater, but it was really better for toast. I also cooked on Sunday nights when we had an early 'tea' of scrambled eggs

and toast, a cup of tea and cold rice pudding. On special occasions I took over the kitchen to 'create', but it seems all I managed to create was a mess. Cooking toffees was the worst mess I have ever been confronted with, and I pity anyone who dares try. Stickjaw toffee came in all shapes and sizes but I can remember it being the blackest, hardest and most awful toffee ever!

Here is a selection of children's ditties, tongue-twisters and jokes about food.

• A Prickly Tongue Twister •

Peter Piper picked a peck of prickly peppers.
Did Peter Piper pick a peck of prickly peppers?
If Peter Piper picked a peck of prickly peppers
Where's the peck of prickly peppers that Peter Piper picked?

Swift ships fetch fresh fish

There was an old man of Calcutta
Who went to sleep in the gutter
But the sun overhead made his head
* into bread*
And melted his nose into butter

Quoted in *New Idea* magazine, 1950

"Toppy Toppa"

Why shouldn't a horse ever
* get hungry?*
Because he always has a bit
* in his mouth!*

Why is a black hen more clever
* than a white hen?*
Because a black hen can lay
* white eggs but a white hen*
* cannot lay black eggs!*

What do geese get when they
** eat too many chocolates?**
Goose pimples!

What do chickens call a test?
An eggsamination!

What is it that you eat every
** day that nobody else eats?**
Your dinner!

Which is the most dissipated,
* cake or wine?*
Cake is often seedy and
* sometimes tipsy but wine*
* is always drunk!*

All riddles from the *Australian Journal*, 1870–90

I eat my peas with honey,
I've done it all my life,
It makes the peas taste funny,
But it keeps them on the knife.

Mrs Ridley who learned it during the 1920s, Nyngan, NSW

Which is the laziest food in
* the sea?*
Oysters, because they are
** always in their beds.**

Why is an oyster a most
* inconsiderate creature?*
Because it has a beard without
* any chin and leaves its bed to*
* be tucked in!*

"PEANUT TWINS"

What are the equivalents of
** good beer, bad beer and**
** ginger beer?**
All slop, all sop and all pop!

When are bakers hard up?
When they knead bread!

Cop the Mickey Mouse hat on the young boy at this 1936 birthday party in Sydney.

At parties for young children, Australians created two ghastly compromises between sweet and savoury: fairy bread, consisting of triangles of white bread (crust removed!) covered with butter and what we knew as 'hundreds and thousands' (now, where did this name come from?). The other dainty treat was nameless and consisted of the same triangle buttered bread but covered with chocolate nonpareils. Other delights included chocolate crackles (made from rice bubbles, cocoa and copha, which was rather like ghee), sponge cakes, cordial and all manner of lollies. Prudent parents refrained from placing dishes of such sweets on the table and presented each child with a parcel of lollies, thus avoiding arbitration at the inevitable 'you've got more than me' squabbles.

With our particular knack of using diminutives we created the word 'lollies' for confectionery. It seems to be a derivative of the word 'lollipop' and originally meant boiled sweets, which were the most common. Early sweet shops offered large jars, chock-a-block full of these boiled sweets. These really were 'gob-stoppers'!

• A Treasury of Australian Lollies •

Rainbow Balls that changed colour when sucked • Slate Pencils that when sucked tasted of aniseed • Traffic Lights (hard toffee discs coloured red, amber, green) • Umbrellas • Aniseed Balls • Sherbets (powder with a stick of licorice included in the pack) • Musk Sticks (pink and later green) • Conversation Hearts • Fried Eggs • Choo Choo bars (licorice/aniseed) • Bubblegum • Licorice Allsorts • Licorice Straps • Licorice Sticks • Chocolate Frogs • White Knights • Fruit Tingles • Tarzan jubes • Orange Squash gums • Bobbies • Kurls • Snowballs • Polly Waffles • Marella jubes • Columbines • Green Frogs • Bullets • Jelly Beans • Honey Bears • Milk Bottles • Wagon Wheels • Violet Crumble bars • Fantails • Jaffas • Hopalong Cassidy bars • Milkos • Black Babies • Cigarette Packs • Fruit Gums • Snakes • Gumballs • Cherry Ripe • Humbugs • Red-Eyes • Nut Kisses • Fairy Floss •

This 'Lifesaver Car' would have been the envy of every little kid when it drove around Sydney as a travelling advertisement for the candy-with-the-hole-in-the-middle. Such larger-than-life promotions were extremely popular; others included a giant loaf of bread, a milk chocolate bar and a huge tin of coffee.

Many of these sweets have moved out of fashion, to be replaced by mass-marketed products, especially the candy bar creations that teenagers seem to enjoy. Advertising of sweets has also changed with a strong emphasis on 'eat this and you'll be popular' campaigns. One of the most popular confectionery campaigns in Australian history must surely be 'it's moments like these you need Minties!', followed closely by 'lollygobbleblissbombs'. Cadbury's chocolate should also get a gong for it's long-running 'glass and a half of milk' campaign. Mention should also be made of the ingenious advertisements for 'keep a Mars Bar in the refrigerator', capitalising on a fad that originated with kids rather than with confectionery manufacturers. The chocolate flake was another lolly we experimented with by placing it in homemade milkshakes, freezing it and — for the mad scientist in us all — trying to cook it. Flakes were also popular as fillings for sandwiches when we were teenagers.

Kids could also torture lollies. I remember a particular craze at Marist Brothers school, Kogarah. The desks had inkwells, and ingenious physics students would fill empty ones with methylated spirits, set them alight and proceed, mid class, to fry Smarties. Once, during the recitation of the rosary, a desk actually caught fire and from then on the brothers kept a vigilant eye on the inkwells. We also tortured licorice straps, the flat one-inch-wide variety, by peeling off the plaited strands one by one. Come to think of it, we seemed to be eating in class all day; the average desk resembled a miniature tuck shop. Small wonder that the 'stand here and put your hand out' caning was such a regular part of our school day.

Some sweets went off the market because they were simply so bizarre. Imagine trying to market a pack of look-alike cigarettes or jubes called 'black babies' in Australia today! Those cigarettes really were a worry. I well remember having one stuck out of the side of my mouth in a very Humphrey Bogart *Casablanca* hey-look-at-me-as-an-adult pose. (Incidentally, why do kids always go for lollies that are shaped like snakes, frogs, bears and other non-food images?)

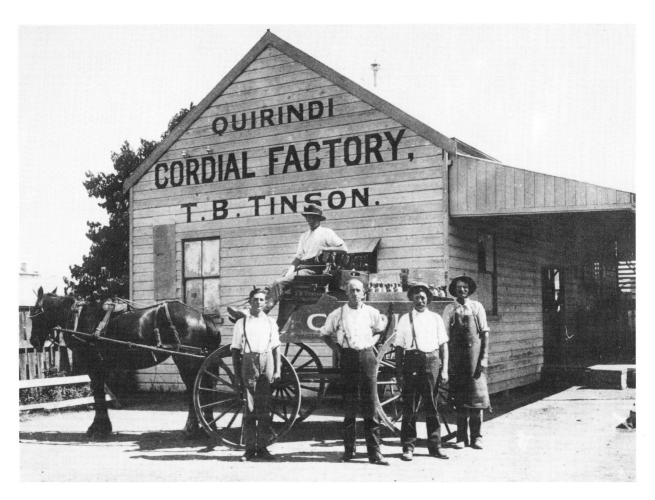

The cordial factory at Quirindi, NSW. Nearly every country town and city suburb had its own cordial factory. Recipes varied but the most popular were the ginger beer and raspberry.

Bubble gum was also popular; and trading cards that came in the packets gave another excuse for buying up big. One of the most popular brands was ML (Maple Leaf) bubble gum, and their collected film star swap cards became all the rage. The blasted stuff used to be everywhere, and was eventually banned from the pictures when big globs of orange sticky stuff were to be found under the seats, on the seats and everywhere else. Anyone who has ever had bubble gum stuck in his or her hair will forever curse the stuff!

There were also kids' food fads. I remember a rather strange 'make your own ice cream' mixture that the milkman used to deliver. It came in a carton that you kept in the freezer and when you had an ice-cream craving, you simply whipped it up in a Mixmaster and refroze it for half an hour. It tasted great at a time when ice cream meant vanilla (there were no other flavours). We also made frozen bananas by poking a paddle-pop stick into a peeled banana and freezing it. Sometimes Mum would dip bananas in chocolate sauce and freeze them on a tray. We'd make our own iceblocks, too, with Passiona, cordial or creaming soda.

The big entertainment event of the week was always Saturday afternoon at the 'fleapit' or local cinema. When we were in polite company, we would call it the flicks or pictures. These were the good old days of Hopalong Cassidy and Spiderman serials, squirming kids and, a little later, the youthful excitement of the 'passion pits'. The lolly counter was never called the 'candy bar'; they certainly didn't sell candy bars! The favourites were undoubtedly the Sherbet Fizzer, an envelope containing a sweet powdery sherbet that you sucked through a licorice straw but that somehow or other

"Yes Sir, it's Peters!"

There's no better Ice Cream made. Exquisite purity, both in manufacture and ingredients, distinguish

PETERS ICE CREAM

(The health food)

Patronise the shops that serve it.

Eat some Peters Ice Cream every day. It is a double delicacy when eaten with a Peters Cake Cone.

PETERS AMERICAN DELICACY
CO. LTD.
George Street, Redfern.

fizzed up your nose. There were also the ever-popular Gumballs, Violet Crumble bars, Rainbow Balls and weird Choo-Choo bars that ended up all over the seat and your face. The Jaffa was popular, probably because of its 'roll 'em down the aisle' ability (the picture palaces had wooden floors!). I realise that I am dating myself when I go back a little further in history, but I can recall getting a free musk stick with my ticket at the Brighton-Le-Sands Roxy picture theatre. The admission price was 1s 6d with a frog-green or shocking-pink musk stick included.

The movies continued to be important. I remember the art cinemas in the 1960s and 1970s — oddly enough, they were called 'cinemas' and not 'the pictures', which continued to show mass-market films. Young would-be intellectuals would buy brewed coffee and croissants and discuss the merits of Fellini, Pasolini and other European film-makers.

Today, our picture theatres are called cinemas and the lolly counter is now the candy bar. The range of sweets is extremely limited, obviously arranged to return the maximum financial return to the cinema chain owners. There are potato crisps, orange cordial drink, chocolate-dipped ice-cream guaranteed to make you very thirsty, popcorn (with one of the highest salt contents in any available snack food), plus a roster of mass-produced super advertised international products such as Mars Bars. The latest innovation is for the 'old favourites', Fantales, Jaffas, or Minties, to be marketed up as 'snack packs' — cellophane-wrapped bags that certainly lack the charm of the original cardboard boxes, not to mention the fact that they are much noisier.

Five years ago I wrote to the two major movie house chains suggesting they include a range of low-sugar health-based sweets and fruit juices, but they responded saying that the public were not ready for such products. A 1990 US-wide survey of what cinema patrons wanted put healthy snack foods in the top spot.

A young couple show off their giant stacked stockings won in a Christmas competition staged by a Paddington, NSW, milk bar and confectionery store. The 'goodies' include dolls, skipping ropes, books, lollies, a toy ship and assorted toys.

It will no doubt come as a shock to many readers to learn that the first milk bar in the entire world was in Sydney. It was opened by Clarence and Norman Burt in 1930 and became an instant success. The Burts also opened a milk bar on the Manly wharf. (On 9 November 1990, the *Sydney Morning Herald* carried a story about the current owner, Marios Hermaridis, who

was quoted as saying, 'I have been here for ten years and I'm still looking for the recipe of Clarrie Burt's hamburger, as well as his invention, the tenpenny Girvana Sling, a mysterious concoction of such appeal that, even fifty years later, elderly visitors to Manly ask for one.') In 1935 Hugh D. McIntosh, an Australian entrepreneur opened a similar establishment in London and the rest is history.

The success of the milk bar can probably be attributed to our desire to copy the American concept of the drugstore but, at the same time, to restrict it to the style and flavour of our British connection. Maybe it was simply a way to sell our excess of milk! Whatever the reason, the milk bar became a very Australian concept, with its long milkshake counter and booth seating. Thankfully, many survive, and we should make sure that they do not disappear, to be completely replaced by the ever-so-impersonal fast food chains.

The milk bars were the social watering hole of young Australia, offering a wide range of snack food, sweets and refreshments. Milkshakes came in all imaginable flavours: peppermint, chocolate mint, double malteds. We also had fresh pineapple crush, ice-cream boats, our Australianised sundaes and, of course, fizzy drinks of all concoctions. Food usually meant a hamburger — a real burger, not one of these Johnny-come lately Wimpys or McDonalds! Real mince, lots of salad, including beetroot, and lots of fried onion and tomato sauce. For variety there was always egg burger and bacon burger or cheese burger. Hot dogs were not particularly popular until they started putting them in the roundabout machines.

Today the milk bar struggles to preserve both its character and its financial basis. Milk bars have been forced to sell all sorts of things, from cigarettes to sandwiches and junk food. Even the good old milkshake seems to have been replaced by pre-packaged flavoured milk products.

A feast of ice cream (from buckets or dixies), at La Perouse, Sydney in 1956.

The Royal Agricultural shows were annual food highlights for thousands of Australians. We would save our pocket money for the show day, where we would eat what our parents dismissed as 'rubbish' but what we viewed as wonder food: potato chips or fries tasted very special to a kid whose only acquaintance with the word takeaway had been the odd slice of devon from the local corner shop. Showbags offered more wondrous offerings with lashings of usually banned lollies which we bought up big and stored as treasures. At the Show kids could be seen lining up for fairy floss (pink or green), toffee apples, giant lollypops, snowies (shaved ice with violently coloured flavourings) and stickjaw toffees. After all this, we went off to turn our stomachs inside out on the roller coasters, spiders and other mechanical monsters of sideshow alley.

I have long been interested in the relationship between food and nutrition. It still appals me what people, especially young mothers, eat during the course of their daily rounds. For about ten years I turned totally vegetarian, mostly on the grounds of humanitarianism rather than diet. I now believe in a healthy mixture of natural foods, but find a good old-fashioned baked dinner pretty hard to refuse, so I don't!

My first association with natural foods came as early as 1964 when I joined the Natural Health Society, founded by L. O. Bailey, a millionaire rag-trader who had developed a pioneering interest in healthy eating during the 1930s. Bailey and his supporters conducted a unique experiment during World War II where they had established a home, called Hopewood, for about sixty orphaned children in the grounds of a beautiful old house in Bowral, in the southern tablelands of New South Wales. Raised on a completely vegetarian diet, the children established world records in dental

Health Week luncheon at Sydney's Trocadero ballroom, 1952. Such lunch menus look far from healthy by today's standards.

An apple a day keeps the doctor away.

and just about every other medical health care. The Natural Health Society still flourishes and the society still maintains various centres, all called Hopewood.

The other states followed Sydney's lead and several chains of bulk food suppliers were established, followed by a network of what became recognised as 'bulk health food' stores, the PDF chain and the Sanitarium health stores being the most successful. As the population became more interested in better diet the health food industry became more visible with natural foods restaurants, speciality magazines, conferences and a growing range of new products.

Attitudes to healthy eating have obviously changed with increased communication, but one only has to stroll down any suburban supermarket aisle to see what the average Australian still consumes. There are seemingly endless stacks of what I would consider 'dead food': frozen vegetables, frozen pies, tinned prepared meals, diet packs and all manner of frozen, dried, tinned foods with an abundance of artificial flavouring, governmentally allowed colouring and enough chemicals to set up a laboratory. I don't buy these prepared foods, my friends claim that they don't, so who does? One thing you can be sure of is that the supermarkets wouldn't stock the products if they didn't sell.

Shopping tends to be influenced by family buying habits and the power of advertising. There are so many product choices in Australian supermarkets, and they're all vying for your dollar. Shoppers usually buy out of habit, convenience and price, but their choices are also influenced by brand loyalty and the effectiveness of recent advertising campaigns. Research shows that effective advertising can convince the general public to select a new brand of breakfast cereal simply by reminding consumers what you think the product should taste like even though they have never tasted it. So much for brand loyalty!

Research also shows that, although we tend to think of ourselves as discerning in our food purchases, shopping is influenced by how much money the shopper has to spend. Certainly we would all like to buy the best available produce, but this may not be economically possible when top grade usually translates into top price. Convenience foods are also a fact of modern life and a growing section of all Australian supermarkets. It is also worth pointing out that although some middle-class people sneer at generic brands and convenience foods, suggesting that only the economically disadvantaged eat such foods, the supermarket shelves of Toorak and Double Bay prove that the people there, too, eat frozen chips, ready-to-heat pies and instant puddings.

7

Here's to the Horse's Arse!

Hooray for Bruce
Hooray at last
Hooray for Bruce
For he's a horse's arse!

And here's an optional extra that's sometimes added:

Don't be misgivin'
Don't be misled
He's not the horse's arse
He's the horse's head

IT'S a reasonable bet that nearly every male adult Australian has been in Bruce's embarrassed shoes; this toast is common throughout Australia as a celebratory song, useful at weddings, football victories, birthdays and any other celebration at which Bruce is being honoured. The 'horse's arse' ditty is often immediately followed by an equally rip-roaring

Why was he (or she) born so beautiful
Why was he born at all
He's no bloody use to any of us
He's no bloody use at all!

And to complete the celebratory trio we usually add a cheer that builds to

Hip hip hooray
For he's a jolly good fellow
And so say all of us

Much has been written about the Australian way of celebrating and, in particular, the way that we conduct ourselves at social gatherings. We have a self-promoted image of 'the blokes are all up forming a scrum around the keg and the sheilas are down the other end of the hall preparing the tucker'. This folk image of ourselves probably stems from the old days when gawky bush workers found themselves, rather uncomfortably dressed, standing in the local hall for a dance or wedding reception. Lacking most social graces, the bush workers bumbled their way through the evening trying to hide their shyness and escaping to the only kind of group camaraderie they knew — to get as 'full as a goog' or 'as drunk as a skunk'.

It is a fact that the average bush worker did not get many opportunities to talk to women, nor did women get much of a chance to talk to men. There

What a challenge! Eat a sticky bun off your own shoulder with your hands behind your back. This photograph was taken on Empire Day, 1918 at Boambee school, NSW.

was much surmising and misinformation on both sides of the fence and when men and women finally did meet some fairly awkward situations could result. Whilst it was almost accepted that the men would get drunk and make fools of themselves, it simply would not do for a woman to get intoxicated.

Australians celebrated not only birthdays, weddings, engagements, christenings, anniversaries, twenty-first birthdays, graduations and bar mitzvahs but Australia Day, Labor Day, Anzac Day and even the racing of the Melbourne Cup. We are said to be one of the most holidayed nations in the world!

Family-based celebrations are firmly tied to tradition, but public celebrations are prone to change. For instance, we no longer celebrate Empire Day (24 May) which, as Queen Victoria's birthday, seemed to be a combination of Guy Fawkes' Day and a toast to the fading British Empire, and which became Bonfire Night or Cracker Night. This exciting tradition was deleted from our festive calendar by the officials, who decided it was dangerous! Tradition, being resilient, has tended to ignore the government bans and cracker night still defiantly exists, but only where there are spaces suitable to build a bonfire. This tends to make it a rather clandestine affair, quite in keeping with Mr Fawkes' original intentions.

When I was a kid growing up in Sydney, Cracker Night was one of the highlights of the year. We saved all our 'odd job' money to buy fireworks such as Catherine wheels, Roman candles, crackerjacks, jumping jacks, throwdowns and, of course, the dreaded double bungers. We would have half a sugar bag of the explosives and an aching desire to blow up something — anything! For days we dreamed of Guy Fawkes blowing up the British Parliament (in our dreams we succeeded!) And as Cracker Night drew nearer, each evening heralded the ear-shattering sound of double bungers exploding in neighbouring letterboxes. We would also seek out our childhood enemies and gangs and, armed to the hilt, would meet for a fullscale bunger war. There were occasional accidents but few were serious (though I still carry a bunger scar right between my eyes where a homemade cannon misfired). Cracker night was also the night of the bonfire and for weeks every neighbourhood prepared and guarded its own. Every day we would cart off some new junk to add to the mountain we had built. There was great rivalry between bonfire makers and the biggest was always best. There was also the guy to be made. These came in all shapes and sizes and were basically fully dressed scarecrows complete with gloves, hats and shoes which were hoisted to the very top of the bonfire. On the evening of 24 May the entire neighbourhood would assemble at about seven, each family bringing a hamper of food and drink. We children were always far too excited to eat and satisfied ourselves with cordial and homemade biscuits. It was an exciting part of our life which, like the British Empire, has all but disappeared.

Christmas, of course, was our other big childhood calendar celebration. Christmas in Australia has always been a confusing celebration — the weather's non-traditional, for a start — but we do seem to be creating our own traditions that have very little to do with reindeers, snowflakes and hot Christmas dinners. Australians have tended to celebrate with a Christmas lunch rather than having food on Christmas Eve or dinner on Christmas Day, and we also seem to be changing the traditional menu.

The first food tradition starts on Christmas Eve when children leave a glass of milk and a slice of fruit cake for Santa Claus. God knows why old St

The annual Christmas party of the GPO in Sydney, 1932. Considering the depressed economy of the day, this seems a well stocked party.

Nicholas would want a glass of milk after all that work, and some Australians prefer to leave a glass of sherry or port. (It makes one think that in years to come Santa may find himself guzzling down a glass of soy milk with his sugarless oatmeal biscuit.) The custom of leaving food for Santa probably came to us from the Swedish tradition of leaving a meal for the spirits protecting the home while the family was out at church.

The Christmas tree is also a very old tradition. This originated as a means of making peace with the harvest gods and ensuring a healthy crop in the coming year. Decorating the tree is a tradition that has changed considerably over the years. In earlier times, Australians would tie sweets and fruit to the tree, but today we use fairy lights and cotton-wool snow. Some peculiar Australians even have reusable aluminium trees.

The Christmas pudding also had its origin as a token to fertility and harvest. The more fruits it contained the more pleasing to the gods it was. Currants were traditionally very important as the grapevine is a sign of peace and plenty. In Australia, we also add small silver coins to the mix and to find one in your slice is an added good luck bonus for the year. As silver sixpences and threepences are no longer available, many cooks have gathered them together for use every year, but this doesn't quite seem the same. Back in the pre-decimal days I remember getting silver coins with the unmistakable sludge of pudding still clinging to them — they persisted in your change for several months.

• Hot Xmas Pudding •

1½ lbs of muscatel raisins, 1¾ lbs of currants, 1 lb of sultanas, 2 lb of finest white moist sugar, 2 lb of breadcrumbs, 2 lbs of finely chopped suet, 8 oz of mixed candied peel, the rind of two lemons. Stone and cut up the raisins, but do not chop them. Pick, wash and dry the currants, cut into thin slices and then mince the candied peel and the rind of the fresh lemons: mix these well together and add one ounce of fresh nutmeg, 1 oz of fresh allspice, ½ oz of bitter almonds: mix these thoroughly. Take the yolk of 20 eggs, the whites of 16. Beat first then separately strain the yolks, add the whites, stir in ¼ pint of good brandy with ½ pint of sherry or good colonial white wine, and mix all thoroughly together. Put no moisture to the pudding but that from the eggs, brandy and wine, and do not in chopping the suet use more flour than is necessary to prevent sticking. Have ready three or four earthenware moulds well buttered. Fill them with the mixture and tie each down closely with a stout new pudding cloth well buttered and floured. The quantity given is too large for an ordinary family pudding; but as the dish is a favourite one for New Year's Day and Christmas Day, it is well to make a good supply and divide. The puddings will require eight hours' steady boiling: when taken out of the pot they should at once be hung in the air, and a saucer placed under each to catch the drippings. When required for use place in boiling water and boil for two hours. At the moment of serving pour a small wine glass of brandy around the pudding, light, and send it to the table in a flame.

From the *Illustrated Sydney News*, 11 December 1875

———— • ————

On the goldfields the miners take great delight in surreptitiously introducing a few small nuggets into the plum-duff — and they do not go round the table after dinner collecting them as some women do the coins. The gold becomes the property of whoever finds it, and it is made into pins, rings and brooches. The habit of salting gold pieces induces a good deal of prospecting, and as the prospectors have to eat up the tailings, it is probably the reason that so many people don't feel very well after the Christmas gorge.

Old quote

Christmas Pudding

4 cups of chopped suet, 2 cups brown sugar, 2 cups raisins, 2 cups sultanas, 2 cups breadcrumbs, 1½ cups flour, 1 cup currants, ½ cup blanched almonds, 8 eggs, 5 pieces of peel, juice and grated rind of two lemons, 1 dessertspoon of ground cinnamon, 1 teaspoon of allspice, ½ teaspoon salt, ¼ pint milk

Mix suet, flour and breadcrumbs and add fruit, almonds, spices, lemon rind and salt. Beat eggs and mix with milk adding to ingredients. Mix well and put mixture into floured cloth and boil for 10 hours. Makes one large and two small puddings.

Mrs Griffiths, Adelaide, SA

Many Australians start or finish their Christmas Day by visiting neighbours for a drink and slice of cake. It is said that every slice of Christmas cake eaten in a friend's house will add an extra month to your life! It is also common to give Christmas cakes as a gift.

Nearly every family appears to have its own secret recipe for Christmas fruit cake. Some contain sherry, some have wholemeal flour, some have no eggs, some are heavy, some light, some are dark, some are not, but all of them are prepared with love and are very rarely store bought.

550 g butter, 625 g flour, 500 g raisins, 125 g almonds, 50 g preserved ginger, 1 heaped teaspoon baking powder, 1 teaspoon cinnamon, 500 g castor sugar, 500 g currants, 125 g mixed peel, 125 g cherries, 3 tablespoons treacle, 12 eggs, 500 g sultanas, 125 g chopped dates, 50 g chopped figs, 3 tablespoons brandy, 1 teaspoon allspice.

Cream butter and sugar. Add eggs one at a time. Add peel and treacle. Sift flour, baking powder and spices together. Mix in fruit with the flour, adding a little at a time. Add brandy then put mixture into a 11-inch cake tin then bake for 6 hours at 125°C.

Mrs M. McDonald, Carlton, Vic

Many Australian women — and the women almost invariably did the cooking for Christmas — made their Christmas cakes weeks in advance. However, considering the number of commercially made Christmas cakes available these days, this seems to be a dying tradition. Home-baked is my choice; there seems to be a bit of added luck associated with any food made at home. Recipes vary from two dozen eggs to no eggs and there are even recipes for Christmas cakes that don't even come near a stove or oven.

• Rich Uncooked Christmas Cake •

1 small cup of soft eating prunes, 1 small cup of seeded raisins, 1 small cup of sultanas, ½ cup of lemon peel, 4 cups of finely rolled malt biscuits, 1 teaspoon coffee essence, ¾ teaspoon cinnamon, ½ cup cherries, ½ cup butter, 2 heaped teaspoons honey, ½ cup sliced almonds, ½ teaspoon almond essence

Mix the chopped fruit and nuts with the spices. Cream butter, honey and essences until soft and creamy. Mix in fruit. Let this mixture stand 2 to 3 hours to soften fruit. Mix in the biscuit crumbs, mixing very thoroughly. Press mixture into a 7-inch tin lined with waxed paper. Put it in the refrigerator or leave in a cool place for a few days. Brush over with the white of egg, ice with almond icing and decorate as desired.

Mrs Deans, St Lucia, Qld

———— • ————

Ross Willis of Fairfield in Sydney told me that his mother cooked several types of fruit cake but the best was one she called the 'stained glass window' Christmas cake, so named because of the stained-glass effect of the glazed fruit and nuts she used.

Many visitors to Australia think we are obsessed with the Queensland pineapple for cooking. It appears in salads, in casseroles, in sweet-and-sour Chinese dishes and even in a dubious version of the Italian pizza that goes by the name of four seasons. Nothing is sacred, not even the Christmas cake!

Christmas in the bush depended on how work was going. Mum would urge Dad to 'take the day off' and he might give in to a day of sheer laziness which, in the bush, was difficult.

Christmas Mince

Peel and core 2 apples and mince 60 g of currants, 60 g of raisins, 60 g of sultanas and 30 g of lemon peel. Add 125 g brown sugar, ½ teaspoon of mixed spice, rind and juice of 1 lemon and 1 tablespoon of sherry. Let all this stand for at least one hour before using but better still make it a few days before Christmas. It improves with age.

Mrs Calbeck, Hindmarsh, SA

Pineapple Christmas Cake

225 g butter, 4 eggs, 4 teaspoons baking powder, 225 g raisins, 125 g cherries, 125 g preserved ginger, 1 teaspoon salt, 1 cup of chopped pineapple, 4 cups flour, 225 g sugar, 2 teaspoons cinnamon, 225 g sultanas, 125 g almonds, 125 g mixed peel, 1 cup pineapple juice

Soak the fruit overnight in the pineapple juice then cream the butter and sugar, adding eggs one by one, and beat well. Add sifted dry ingredients and fruit alternately. Bake for 4 hours at 145°C.

Mrs Coffey, Hawthorne, Qld

These old blokes are having Christmas dinner at the Lidcombe Hospital in 1955.

Hop-beer, ginger-beer, and honeymead are also made, and stored away in kegs and bottles for the Christmas celebration. 'Sugarbags' are plentiful in many parts of the bush, and a good nest or two is usually left for December, when the trees are felled and the bees robbed. The beer is made from the comb after the honey has been drained out of it, sarsaparilla is another extensively-made drink, the vines growing plentiful among the ranges.

On Christmas Eve the boys go out with guns for scrub turkeys, pigeons and ducks. Often they spend the whole day shooting in the scrubs, and round the swamps and lagoons; and they come home well-laden with game. All hands and the cook turn up after tea and pluck the birds. The bushman's table is rarely without game at this time.

Edward Sylvester Sorenson, *Life in the Australian Backblocks, 1869–1939*

The main Christmas meal in early Australia was apparently the evening meal on Christmas Day. It was a version of the traditional British festive meal, complete with various baked meats, gravies, pies and all the trimmings. Dessert was a series of heavy and sweet puddings covered with glazes, sherry and pouring custards.

However, to many early bushmen Christmas would have passed without acknowledgment. In his diary of 1844 explorer Ludwig Leichhardt wrote: 'Dec. 25th. We returned to Brown's Lagoon and entered our camp just as our companions were sitting down to their Christmas dinner of suet pudding and stewed cockatoos. The day was cloudy and sultry; we had a heavy thunderstorm on Christmas Eve.'

We eventually accepted the fact that Christmas in Australia is slap bang in the middle of summer and all the traditional stodge was totally out of place on our tables. Australians changed the main meal to become the Xmas lunch and we also changed what we served.

• Welcome to Xmas •
By a new chum 1865

An Australian welcomes as hearty
as true
Though we light not the candle nor
kindle the log
If far from old Britain, we're
Englishmen true
And yet can dispense with her cold,
sleet and fog
The sun is as hot as a good yule fire
In fact rather warmer than heart
can desire
Except to those — sad mosquitoes —
Whose fretful buzzing makes one
perspire
Oh, we've lots of amusement at
Christmas time
Though we lack the wits and mummers
Tis it's true we can't skate and our boys
can't slide
But sixpenny ices are stunners
And as to good cheer, we've stout, ale
and beer prices

Warranted high and quality low and
if more to keep Christmas
It needful appear wine, colonial, a bob
or so
I must confess
Our style's more extensive than words
can express.

For 'tis boots of buckskin, pipe-layered
white
Spider web, peg tops and coat as light
Puggarees damp and spectacles dark
Helmets of pith and hats of cork
Umbrellas of every conceivable hue
Black and white, green, brown and blue
Not to keep off either rain or dew
But to lesson a little the terrible stew
That the glowing sun and hot north wind
Which is sure to burn and is apt to blind
Inflict upon Antipodean mankind

Australian Journal, Christmas 1865

In a country town on the southern road into Sydney there was a man named Madden who kept the pub. The Saturday before Christmas, a couple of bushies came into the bar and proceeded to sell raffle tickets for a suckling pig that they had killed and trussed. The price of the tickets started at ten bob and later in the afternoon dropped to five bob and even later they dropped to two and six each. When they couldn't sell any more tickets they asked Madden to draw the lucky ticket out of a hat. The prize was won by a young chap who said that he lived in a boarding house and would rather sell the pig for five quid. The publican said he'd take it and he took it out and put it in the kitchen refrigerator. There was a retired butcher living at the pub and the publican asked him if he would cut the porker up so they could have roast pork that evening. After he got the pig out the butcher declared, 'This is the strangest pig I have ever seen! It's got no bloody tail!' The story soon got around and sure enough the publican became known as 'Wombat Madden'.

Recorded from Arthur Dally, Townsville, Qld, 1973

In a northern New South Wales town there lived a Pom who earned his living by doing odd building jobs. He'd taken a job on the outskirts of town working for a woman who bred geese. Like a lot of Poms, he used to wear big baggy, wide-legged shorts known as Bombay bloomers. Well, on this day, shortly before the Christmas holiday, he was nailing some timber on the back shed. As usual, there were geese wandering all over the place when all of a sudden a goose, seeing something dangling up the trouser leg grabbed it and began to swallow. The Pom quickly downed his hammer, grabbed the goose by the neck and wrestled to get his property back! This proved to be very difficult as a gander's teeth slope backwards. After a brief and bitter struggle the man was forced to call out to the woman for help. She tried in vain and eventually said, 'It's no use, I'll have to go into the house and get a carving knife to cut its throat'. Alarmed the Pommy screamed, 'For God's sake don't do that, I don't know how much he's got down his throat!'. Eventually they decided to choke the gander to death and eventually freed the badly cut Pom. The woman drove him into town and the doctor had to insert several stitches, which caused great amusement throughout the town. To the Pom it was a very sore point!

From Arthur Dally, Townsville, Qld, 1973

Ginger Beer

Boil 5 oz bruised ginger in three quarts of water for half an hour. Add 5 lb white sugar, 1 gill of lemon juice and ¼ lb of honey. Strain the liquid through a cloth. When cold add a quarter of an egg white and a tablespoon of essence of lemon and let it stand for four days (or three if the weather is very hot). Bottle and cork. It will keep for approximately three months but is liable to explode as the pressure builds.

Australian Journal, 1880

A travelling salesman found himself in the outback. He stayed at a typical country pub where the evening meal was the same night after night: cold corned mutton and potatoes. After the fourth night the salesman asked the waitress, 'Could I please have some pickles?' 'Hang on,' she replied and strolled over to the kitchen door where she yelled out, 'Hey, cook, there's a silly coot in here who reckons it's Christmas!'

A common Australian response to a seemingly impossible request is, 'What do you think it is? Bush Christmas?' implying that certain things are only available on very special occasions and this isn't one of those days.

Many Australians have found themselves celebrating Christmas far from home during wartime. This poem is typical of the general sentiment expressed.

• Christmas at Camp Kaos 1944 •

'Twas Christmas day at Kaos and all
were out to survive,
Stood to in their trenches and thought
of their wenches
'Till damned near a quarter to five
Later they lined up for breakfast, those
boys they call
'Ikes' Marines'
The cook had tried to prepare some good
Christmas fare
With burgoo and tins of baked beans.

'And what's for dinner?' arose the cry
'Bully, a famed Christmas dish.'
But you're not afraid, just take a
grenade
And blow up a panful of fish
So while other folks are enjoying
roast duck
With lashings of seasoning and peas
We'll stuff our gullet with freshly
caught mullet
To the tune of the roar of the seas.

Stan Briggs, Haberfield, NSW, recorded 1986

My father always had a glass of this first thing on Christmas morning, possibly as a lining for the diverse things that would follow.

Bring one cup of milk to the boil. Add one tablespoon of sugar and one quarter teaspoon of vanilla. Remove from the stove and allow to cool. Beat the yolks of two eggs until the colour of lemon. Combine eggs with milk and stir then return to the heat bringing it to the boil but do not boil. Allow to cool then add half a cup of rum and stir well. The eggnog is ready to go.

The trifle seems to be a little bit of this and little bit of that — or whatever else you fancy! Here's a favourite family recipe.

1 sponge cooked in a Swiss roll tin, 1 packet of port wine jelly, 60 ml of sherry, 60 ml of port, juice of one large lemon, Maraschino cherries, 450 ml boiling water, 4 bananas

Cut the sponge into fingers and brush with the combination of sherry and port and place these around the sides of a springform pan. Cut the remaining sponge into triangles and place these around the base of the tin, sprinkling with the remainder of the booze. Arrange some of the bananas (which have been soaked in the lemon juice) on the bottom of the pan. Pour a cupfull of the half set jelly over the sponge and fruit base and set it in the refrigerator. After about an hour pour in the rest of the bananas and jelly and put back into the refrigerator. Now we have to make the custard part of the trifle: beat together 2 eggs and 125 g of sugar and place in a double boiler with 300 ml of milk, a teaspoon of vanilla and a mixture of 1 dessertspoon of gelatine and 1 tablespoon of hot water. Cook all this and stir until the mixture is nice and thick. Pour this into the jelly and allow to set. When you're ready to serve, top it off with whipped cream, the dreaded cherries, some almonds and whatever else you fancy, Yum!

When I was a kid in the 1950s and 1960s Christmas lunch always meant chicken. We ate beef and lamb every week, but chicken was considered a special festive food. For many years we had hot chicken with baked potatoes and gravy plus a giant leg of baked ham. This was followed by apple pie, a hot fruit pudding with custard and, of course, lollies. The table was always decorated with flowers, bon bons and candles and there were funny paper hats for everyone at the table. As a large family we usually had a table for the adults and another for the children, but everyone, young and old, had to have bon bons and a hat. The family dog would also have a special Christmas lunch. Now chicken is no longer considered a luxury or festive food and speciality poultry and game have taken its place. Turkey, duck and designer poultry are now served on the Christmas table.

The Christmas ham was also an important part of the festive season. Great care was taken in the purchase, with many butchers advising: 'Order your Xmas ham now!' as if they were to be in short supply. Christmas ham clubs were also popular, whereby the ham was paid off over a number of weeks prior to the big day. Despite the fact that my Mother was Jewish, we always had a glazed leg of ham, a whopping great big thing that hardly fitted in the refrigerator. After Christmas lunch the ham was carefully wrapped in either cheesecloth or a tea-towel which was supposed to prevent the ham from 'sweating'. We grew to hate it, sitting there in the refrigerator defying any of us to take yet another meal from its bone. We had it on sandwiches, on salad, fried with eggs, minced in mashed potatoes and even coated in egg and breadcrumbs. We always ended up throwing it out as nothing seemed to stop it from eventually 'sweating to death'. We were thankful Christmas only came once a year!

In 1965, Christmas Day was a real scorcher and topped 100 degrees Fahrenheit. Mum in the kitchen, preparing a full hot lunch, fainted from the heat. That was the last hot Christmas meal we ever had, and Christmas lunch became a cold lunch that included a far more acceptable banquet of seafood, cold meats, salads and fruits. As a salute to tradition we retained the hot Christmas pudding but I was always more interested in the port wine trifle and the huge slices of iced watermelon. Nowadays my Christmas lunch tends to be a picnic luncheon open to family, strays and waifs and it alternates between a lavish spread in the backyard and on one of Sydney's many beautiful beaches.

Xmas Apple Drink

Boil six or seven Pippin apples cut into six or eight pieces in half a gallon of water until they become soft. Strain through a sieve and sweeten with honey or sugar. Cool and drink.

In December, 1888, the *Boomerang* magazine suggested the following menu as suitable for an Antipodean repast.

• SOUPS •
MACARONI OR OXTAIL

• FISH •
FRIED MULLET OR BOILED BREAM AND PARSLEY SAUCE

• POULTRY •
ROAST TURKEY AND BREAD SAUCE OR BOILED FOWL AND HAM

• MEAT •
ROAST BEEF OR VEAL
VEGETABLES
MARROW, FRENCH BEANS, POTATOES

• PUDDINGS •
PLUM PUDDING AND CUSTARD, BLANC MANGE AND APRICOTS

• DESSERTS •
ALMONDS AND RAISINS, ORANGES, BANANAS, MUSCATELS AND
WATERMELONS, APPLES AND GRAPES

• BEVERAGES •
TEA, COFFEE, LEMON SQUASH

This table at the Motor Accessory Ball, 1937, seems more appropriate to the Native Plants Society Ball. Note the extra-long-necked beer bottles.

Queen Victoria's son, Prince Alfred, the Duke of Edinburgh, visited Australia in 1867, and was scheduled to attend a Christmas banquet in Melbourne. This was a dinner attended by thousands of freeloading Melburnians. It seems to have been given a rather bad press.

• The Free Banquet at Melbourne •
(Parody: Four-and-Twenty Blackbirds)

Sixty thousand loafers, all jammed
together
At the monster banquet, in very
hot weather
Sixty thousand hungry brutes,
gnashing their teeth
Eager to drink the wine and gorge
the roast beef
Sixty thousand savages, dirty
and greasy
Dr Louis Laurence Smith, clean
and uneasy

Sixty thousand drunken louts,
roaring out 'Wine!'
A squadron of troopers drawn up
in line
Hundreds of pretty girls, amidst these
wretches huddled
Sixty thousand Christians, stupid
and fuddled
Wasn't this a picture to make the
doctor wince
Wasn't this a dainty dish to set
before the prince?

From the *Laughing Jackass,* a satirical magazine,
Mitchell Library, Sydney

Most large department stores had a ballroom available for hire. This photograph was taken at the Blaxland Gallery, Farmers Ltd, Sydney in 1937. The packet of Capstan cigarettes implies that this is a pretty swish crowd.

To make custard, take a pint and a half of milk, and put it on the fire in a clean saucepan; when it comes to the boil, add some grated lemon-peel, a couple of peach-leaves, a pinch of salt, and two ounces and a half of powdered white sugar. Let the milk simmer until it has acquired the flavour of the lemon-peel and peach-leaves, but keep stirring it all the time or it will burn. Use a wooden spoon for this purpose. Have the yolks of eight eggs ready beaten up, put them into the milk, and keep stirring until the custard becomes thick. If it boils or becomes too hot it will curdle.

New South Wales also decided to celebrate the Prince's visit with a picnic at the northern beach resort of Clontarf. By all reports it was 'straight out of Mrs Beeton's illustrious book' with a menu of oysters and stout, chicken, lobster and champagne. Unfortunately the meal became a fiasco when a local Irishman decided to take a potshot at the Prince. He was whisked away with a superficial wound in the shoulder and the remaining guests decided to toast him by demolishing eleven hundred magnums of champagne and nearly eight hundred bottles of beer.

Custard played a large part in sweetening up the early Australian festive palate. The best known brand was undoubtedly Foster Clark's Custard Powder, advertised with the words, 'Many Australian homes appreciate this economical luxury'. An economical luxury indeed! Keeping an eye on the custard was a tough job for any child and the temptation to take a wee spoonful was too great to withstand. Personally I preferred my custard a day old and straight from the refrigerator and, if I was lucky, complete with a few hefty lumps!

———— • ————

Weddings are another cause for high celebration, and probably one of the most custom- and superstition-influenced celebrations in our society. On such an auspicious occasion, what bride or groom wants to risk bad luck by wearing the wrong colour or having the wrong foods at the reception?

Wedding receptions in early Australia were very casual; giant tables were laid out with food and wine and everyone in the neighbourhood seemed welcome to participate. By all accounts such weddings saw hordes of pioneers descending on the tables eating away like a locust plague and then leaving with enough meats to feed the family for another week. As the population of the colony increased the style of the wedding reception changed, becoming somewhat more exclusive. However, it is still an extraordinarily expensive exercise, especially for the bride's family, as tradition holds that the reception be hosted by the bride's family as a dowry. It is a widespread custom to shower the bride and groom with rice as they leave the church as a symbol of plenty — may your pantry always be full!

A great example of the wedding cake decorator's art.

Remember me over the water
Remember me over the lake
Remember me at your wedding
And send me a piece of the cake!

A common autograph book entry

The most important food at the Australian wedding is the cake; like the Christmas cake it is made of fruit and nuts, symbolising fertility. The cake is traditionally covered with white marzipan icing and tradition states that the bride should not be involved in making it. The first cut of the cake should be made by the bride and groom, who jointly hold the knife. All guests partake of the cake as a sign of good luck to the newlyweds. Some Australian weddings also have a 'groom's cake' which is usually a dark chocolate cake: pure white for the bride and devilish dark for the groom! Wedding cakes are always lavishly decorated and decorations may include a miniature bridal couple, a grapevine symbolising harmony and frosted grapes for fecundity.

Celebrating in Australia usually means a cake being baked. Because of our climate our cakes are lighter than those of colder Europe. As with all

traditions, our cake names tell stories. Here is a partial list culled from the Bundaberg Branch of the Country Women's Association Cookery Book (fifth edition, undated):

Hinkler Cake, Three Minute Cake, Brown Elsie Cake, Brunswick Cake, Chessboard Cake, Daisy Hill Cake, Economical Festivity Cake, Fail-Me-Never Cake, Feather Cake, Jazz Cake, Jenny Lind Cake, Jew Cake, Judge Cake, Marble Cake, Pink and White Cake, Prune Cake, Rainbow Cake, Sand Cake, Simnel Cake, Velvet Cake, Watermelon Cake, Yankee Cake, Bachelors' Buttons, Date Cuddles, Date Dainties, Digger Nuts, Fairy Delights, Goblin Gems

Cake shaping and decorating were extremely popular in Australia and most of the early retail mail order catalogues and women's magazines offered extensive 'cake decorating aids'.

The twenty-first birthday in Australia still signifies a 'coming of age' and traditionally the time to be given the key of the door' (although the legal age of adulthood is now eighteen). There are no obvious traditional foods, the birthday party always includes a lavishly decorated cake, plus an extensive range of food. Most twenty-first celebrations are held at home with a mix of family and friends. Quite often the cake is shaped like a key and this song is sung while the cake is cut:

> *She's twenty-one today*
> *Twenty-one today*
> *She's got the key of the door*
> *Never been twenty-one before*
> *We'll shout hip hip hooray*
> *She's a jolly good fellow*
> *She's twenty one today*

This monster cake fed 10,000 Albury school children to mark the anniversary of explorers Hume and Hovell's appearance in the district in 1824. Someone snapped a picture and made it into a postcard.

Pavlova

Beat three egg whites stiff and add 1 cup of sugar, then 1 heaped teaspoon of cornflour, ¼ teaspoon of baking powder, 1 teaspoon vanilla and 1 teaspoon of vinegar. Place on greased white paper (the cold side). Bake for one hour in a very low oven of 110°C.

A twenty-first birthday cake, 1939, taken at Elizabeth Bay. The birthday girl was Miss Jean Gillespie and the report states that 'toasts were raised at midnight with the cutting of the cake'.

There was a time when 'party food' meant sausage rolls, cocktail 'little willy' frankfurts (with tomato sauce), miniature meat pies, cubed cheddar cheese and water biscuits. More substantially party food tended to be beef stroganoff or chicken mornay and if you were really lucky both dishes served on the one plate! Fortunately times have changed and, like the rest of our cuisine, the party food menu is changing to a more sophisticated and edible assortment.

Some of the most significant traditions related to food are, of course, closely related to religion: the fasting period of Lent, Shrove Tuesday, Jewish Kosher cookery, Muslim Halal cookery, etc. I was raised in a family that had a Jewish and an Irish Roman Catholic heritage so I have an excuse for total confusion. I remember being disappointed when the Pope relaxed the 'no meat' on Fridays ruling as I had always looked forward to our Jewish style of fish cookery — I had a two-way bet!

———— • ————

I once heard of a young woman in the bush who had led a rather sheltered life and had never heard about Jesus Christ, let alone 'no meat Fridays'. Well, her father sent her over to a neighbours station on Good Friday; he urgently needed a small tractor part. When she arrived at the station homestead she was invited to stay for lunch and the hostess explained that 'they would be eating fish because Christ died today'. When she finally returned home she told her parents that they had eaten fish because one of the neighbours and unfortunately died earlier in the day!

Yarn printed in the *Colonial Magazine*, 1921

Australians have always called a spade a spade so it is hardly surprising that we take an irreverent attitude towards saying grace. Meant as an offering to God for gracious gifts, etc., these Australian-style ditties are gems of the art:

They don't look too happy about being photographed at this bush birthday party at Walgett, NSW in 1935.

Two, four, six, eight
Bog in don't wait.

See my finger
See my thumb
Look out tummy
Here it comes!

Hail Mary full of grace
All her knickers made of lace
One word's as good as ten
Bog in. Amen!

Roll your eyes around the table
Fill your belly while you're able

Nancy Cavanagh, 1990

One word's as good as ten
Get ready. Amen!

Eat away, chew away
Munch and bolt and guzzle,
Never leave the table till
You're full up to the muzzle

Norman Lindsay, *The Magic Pudding*

Not for my sake
Not for your sake
But for God's sake —
I give this bread to you.
But for my sake
And for gawd's sake —
Put some butter on it!

And one final ditty to be uttered when one burps:

Pardon me for being so rude
It was not me, it was my food
It just came up to say hello,
And now it's gone back down below

Mark Cavanagh, Sydney, 1990

8

Let's Eat Out!

I humbly dips me lid
I dips it dinky-di
To the man who orders chips
When the menu says 'French fries'

Clem Parkinson, Melbourne, 1983

EATING out is a relatively new idea for Australians. It became possible and fashionable around the turn of the century. We certainly had plenty of 'eating houses' in early Australia, but these were restaurants of necessity rather than convenience. The colonial cities had numerous taverns and cafes and the rural centres had shanties that served the pioneer equivalent of the 'counter lunch'. We had plenty of pioneer 'fast food' too, with saveloy sellers, piemen and all manner of hot and cold foods sold by street hawkers.

For many Australians, the first experience of eating out is the barbecue. It is difficult to trace where the term, or its abbreviation BBQ, originated but the invitation to a barbecue or 'barbie' as it is affectionately known, is rarely refused. It is suspected that the word originated from the Haitian *barbacoa*, meaning a framework of sticks for smoking or roasting food.

The Australian barbecue traditionally means an out-of-doors cooked meal that could include: sausages, chops, steak or chicken, buttered bread, tomato sauce, potato salad and coleslaw, followed by watermelon and a good cup of tea. All courses are served with iced beer from the esky. Many Australians now barbecue on smart gas convection barbecues and eat satays, trout and squab, followed up with a French gateau washed down with a crisp dry white wine.

When Australians cook on a real barbecue it must be a grill or piece of chicken wire over a blazing fire. None of that pussyfootin' Japanese hibachi nonsense for the true Australian! All the better if the temperature is as hot as Hades and never mind if the snags and chops are a bit burned.

An Englishman was invited to a typical outback barbecue but he wasn't enjoying it one bit. 'Look old fellow,' he whinged to his half-tanked host, 'I don't know about you coves but I simply cannot stand these flies'. 'Well', drawled the Australian, opening another tinny, 'Why don't you piss off and come back tomorrow — there'll be a new lot then!'

One of the greatest joys of the Australian barbie must certainly be the attraction of the flies, especially the bush blowies! Songwriter Eric Bogle documents the full catastrophe in his hilarious 'Barbecue Song':

• Barbecue Song •

*When the summer sun shines brightly
   on Australia's happy land
Round countless fires in strange attire,
   you'll see many solemn bands
Of glum Australians watching their
   lunch go up in flames
By the smoke and smell, you can
   plainly tell, it's barbie time again.*

*The Scots eat lots of haggis, the French
   eat snails and frogs,
The Greeks go crackers over their
   moussaka, and the Chinese love
   hot dogs,
Welshmen love to have a leek, the Irish
   love their stew
But you just can't beat the half-cooked
   meat at an Aussie barbecue*

*There's flies stuck to the margarine, the
   bread has gone rock-hard,
The kids are fighting, the mossies are
   biting, 'Who forgot the Aeroguard?'
There's bull ants in the esky, and the
   beer is running out,*

*And what you saw in Mum's coleslaw —
   you just don't think about.*

*And when the barbie's over and
   homeward way you wend
With a queasy tummy on the family
   dunny, many lonely hours you spend,
You might find yourself reflecting, as
   many often do,
Come rain or shine, that's the very last
   time, that you'll have a barbecue!*

The snags are sizzling on a 1958 makeshift barbecue in a big backyard.

Eric Bogle's barbecue song always conjures up the image of a *National Lampoon* Chevy Chase-type situation comedy complete with barking dogs, children who simply will not stand still, a swarm of very-hungry flies and food that refuses to cook. There are now several barbecue supermarkets around Australia who will gladly sell you enough equipment to make your cookout a nightmare. There are several types of cooking units, fold-up furniture, eskies (or chilly-bins if you're a Kiwi), cooking equipment, aprons, insect repellent and a zillion other necessary products. It's enough to make an old swaggie laugh into his pannikin.

Interestingly enough, the European and Asian migrants are teaching us the real joys of outdoor cookery — none of this burnt snags and chops nonsense for their sophisticated palates. Visit any main city beach or park and you'll find family after family of non-Anglo Saxon Australians enjoying a picnic with very few hassles.

The second eating-out experience of the average Australian is at the local 'Chinese' restaurant. The Chinese first came to Australia in the goldrush days and stayed to find a much more lucrative 'gold' in chicken chow mein and chop suey. It has often been said that the Chinese food in Australia is a far cry from the noble cooking traditions of Imperial China. This might have been true of yesterday's Chinese restaurants, but today's Australia can certainly claim some of the best Chinese restaurants outside China or Hong

Kong. We also have excellent Vietnamese, Thai, Indonesian, Malay, Indian, Japanese and Burmese restaurants catering for what seems to be a growing interest in Asian foods. These create a new food folklore and their popularity has almost eliminated the 'watch out for pussycat in your chow mein' mentality that thrived a few years back. But what I call 'goldrush fake Chinese cuisine' persists in the Chinese restaurants to be found in the clubs of country towns. The menus are predictable, featuring glutinous dishes that defy description and taste. To be fair, it appears that most of these bland Chinese recipes were created to appease the then bland taste buds of early Australians and I seriously doubt if the kitchen staff would eat these dishes. Eating Chinese in Australia used to be known as 'going to the Chows for a feed' — thankfully this phrase is now disappearing along with chop suey and Asian cuisine is now our number one eating out experience.

Folklore plays a major role in providing a platform for our communal fears in regard to food and many stories are told of Chinese restaurants. Maybe this racism is left over from the days of the goldfields when the Chinese would cradle the mullock heaps and find specks of gold missed by the lazy diggers; maybe it simply came from our suspicion of anything that didn't look like roast beef and three vegetables. Maybe it was because Chinese food seemed to contain ingredients unfamiliar to Europeans. Whatever the reason, the stories abound of cockroaches in the chop suey or a mouse tail in the chow mein.

There are also stories of non-animal additives such as screws, cigarette butts, nails, glass slivers and even a condom. Logical explanations tend to favour a disgruntled employee who was 'trying to get back at his boss'. Whilst such vicious 'public' contamination is not likely, it is certainly not unknown for workers to have a 'bit of fun' at the expense of the boss. (Tales of workers peeing into the chocolate mix, etc, are commonly circulated. Related to this is the customer's fear that in rejecting a badly cooked restaurant meal it will inevitably go back into the kitchen where the cook will, at best, spit on it and send it out again!)

The recent arrival of immigrants from Vietnam, Thailand and Cambodia has sparked new urban myths related to Asians being suspected of stealing and eating household pets. Tellers swear that they 'know someone who lost a pet' or found 'evidence in the Asian family's garbage' or even 'read it in the paper'. Tied to this myth are stories like this one: a couple went to a Vietnamese restaurant in the Sydney suburb of Fairfield and asked if their dog could wait in the backyard. The waiter thought they wanted him to cook the dog, which he did, and served it to the couple. This is clearly a myth, but a vicious story in the hands of a racist is a dangerous tool. In passing it is worth mentioning that in the 1950s and 1960s such racism and myth-telling was aimed at the Italians and Greeks and, we now know, the myths have tended to disappear as the migrants became part of the fabric of Australian society.

Our close relationship with Asia has generously contributed to our cuisine. We now find many Asian foods on our supermarket shelves, including tofu, soy milk, spices and even Asian specialty vegetables. The wok is now more common than the pressure cooker.

Anyone who really wants to be excited by our multicultural society, especially its contributions to the kitchen, need only visit Darwin's famous weekly open air village marketplace, where visitors can stroll past stall-holders who are cooking up a global storm. Food includes Tibetan, Malay, Greek, regional Chinese, Vietnamese, Korean, Thai, Cambodian and Dutch, and the sights, smells and sounds are tantalising and encourage a real food feast. This market has been a huge success financially, but also as a

Welcome to the Blue Room Cafe, Glen Innes, NSW, in 1938. This looks like a fine establishment complete with rolled jam sponge, hand-made chocolates, fruit cakes and layered sponge delights.

multicultural public relations campaign. It is a pity that the seemingly ferocious 'stickler for the rules' brigade of local council health departments couldn't take a more sensible approach to such out-of-doors dining for our southern cities.

Most migrants who come to Australia are amazed at the lack of outdoors eating venues. We have some of the world's best weather, wonderful beachfronts and equally wonderful produce, but the mere thought of a table on the street sends waves of shock horror over the above-mentioned protectors of the public health. These regulations must be changed, and the sooner the better.

Cafes are one significant improvement for which we can thank our European settlers. The English tea house seems to have disappeared to be replaced with coffee shops offering cappuccino, mocca, latte, Vienna, short black, long black and Spanish cordado. The raisin toast, tinned spaghetti or cheese on toast of yesterday's world seem to have been replaced with croissants, bagels and fruit toasts. Many of these cafes take great pride in their coffee making ability and specialist cafes attract loyalty similar to that of the most diehard beer drinker. There is a real skill in making a good espresso coffee and once discovered the instant and the insipid are best forgotten.

Restaurant dining in Australia can be a real hit and miss experience. There are some excellent restaurants and some real shockers. As a nation we have Australianised several international dishes that provide us with what we called 'international cuisine'. This was usually an excuse for serving a classic European dish with a serving of pineapple pieces. Here's a handful that will give you the general idea (complete with their Australianised spelling!): strawberries romanoff, black forest cake, Hungarian paprika schnitzel, Hawaiian ham steak with pineapple, veal *vol au vent* (in a pasty flour sauce that would flatten any respectable Frenchman), filet Mexican

Cafe society in full swing. As Australians became more relaxed about eating out, they readily adopted the European concept of using a cafe for ambience and recreation, not just the place for a quick meal.

covered with chilli con carne and the ultimate French menu of garlic bread, paté, French onion soup, duck *a l'orange* followed by crêpes suzette and profiterolles. Seek and you will find far better offerings!

The Australian milk bar cafe has a long tradition. To my mind they were always owned and operated by Greeks who continually wiped the counter with swaying motions designed to leave a smear on the laminex. As there were hardly any Greeks in Australia until the late forties it seems as if they must have jumped off the wharf at Sydney's Circular Quay and immediately bought up every available milk bar in sight! The blighters also must have changed the names from 'Bluebell Cafe', 'The Empire' and 'Railway Refreshment Cafe' to what we have today — 'Acropolis Cafe', 'Paragon Milk Bar and Cafe', 'Adelphi Cafe' and 'The Athenian'. Like the Chinese restaurants the Greeks created a cuisine to appeal to the then bland Australian palate — mixed grills, omelettes, pie with vegetables, sausages and mashed potatoes, etc. Thankfully these too are changing and the owners are now starting to introduce souvlakia, moussaka, yeeros and Greek roasts. Australians, always ready with a derogatory put-down, call it 'going to have a feed at the greasy' or simply 'going to the Greeks'. Thank goodness they came!

Melbourne, recognised as the third largest Greek city in the world, has a thriving Greco-Australian tradition and lots of marvellous Greek eating houses. The 'Greekness' of Melbourne is quite apparent to the visitor and especially inner-city suburbs like Richmond where Greek shops, restaurants, clubs, churches and pastry shops are highly visible. I recall several years ago when I visited my first Greek club which really was an upstairs 'out of sight out of mind' Greek restaurant that happened to serve alcohol illegally. The late Declan Affley, that great singer, musician and drinker, had been performing at Frank Trayner's club and, as was his want, Declan declared that we were all 'going up to the Greeks' where he 'knew a good man'. It was a rare sight indeed with the evocative sounds of Greek music, the clatter of plateloads of moussaka, baked lamb and pastries and, of course, the illegal but highly welcome illicit bottles of beer. I later discovered that these Greek clubs are common right across Australia and most of them were also known as places for after-hours drinking and sometimes gambling.

As a teenager without much money I searched Sydney for inexpensive places to eat. My two favourites were the natural health restaurant in Liverpool Street where a few dollars would buy gigantic salads, spinach pies and fruit salads, and the other was an Elizabeth Street Greek eatery called the Minerva. At the Minerva $3.95 would buy more than a touch of the Mediterranean: chicken lemon soup, a moussaka the size of half a house brick, a whole quartered raw onion and a bowl of Kalamata olives. Both noble establishments have since disappeared, but are not forgotten.

The last eating-out experience (for many young Australians, the first eating-out destination) is the local fast food outlet. Kentucky Fried Chicken, McDonald's, Pizza Hut, Taco Belle's and Red Rooster all specialise in offering fast food that can be eaten as take-away or, in most cases, at the associated restaurant. The food is bite-sized and comes with an array of highly pro-cessed side serves such as chips, mashed potatoes and gravy, coleslaw, baked potato, etc, plus tiny plastic forks and a paper napkin. Service is designed to be anonymous and fast, fast, fast. One chain even offers to refund your money if the service is slow. These chains also serve Coca-Cola or Pepsi and are continually advertising 'special' inducements for the children that range from toys to bonus fries. These fast food chains now cover the country like a network from Darwin to Tasmania and even the country towns, where one would imagine that the locals really weren't in that much of a hurry! Sadly the spread of fast food chains has meant the death-knell for the typical Australian hamburger, but that's progress.

Environmentally concerned Australians have recently waged a war against many fast-food corporations to reduce the amount of litter they create, especially the non-recyclable packaging that has become a scourge on our beaches. The chains have responded positively to this pressure. Australians refer to this type of convenience food as 'junk food' but this does not stop them consuming millions of dollars of burgers, chickens and other kinds of convenience food every year.

I remember the launch of Kentucky Fried Chicken in Australia when we agreed to 'let the Colonel do the cooking'. In fact, I attended and sang at a reception for the Colonel and his wife and he even sang 'My Old Kentucky Home'. Little did I think that this new food would sweep the country with such enthusiasm eventually replacing the traditional hamburger shop that had been such a part of my youth. A few years ago, Melbourne songwriter Clem Parkinson, never lost for a word, wrote a song that appealed to Australians to stop the spread of the mighty chain.

Colonel Sanders Kentucky Fried Chicken
It's finger-licking crook
The way that our country is being
* 'fowled up'*
From Sydney to Tallarook
Our whole way of life is beginning
* to sicken*
It really isn't a joke

We should send a message direct to
* the Yanks*
Have Colonel Sanders reduced to
* the ranks*
Send back his chickens and tell him
* 'No thanks'*
We want to be freed from his yoke —
And we don't want Pepsi or Coke!

Eating out in today's Australia, then, can mean a variety of dining experiences as Australia now has a truly cosmopolitan cuisine. The migration programmes have resulted in excellent urban and regional cuisine. It is possible to find high standards and interesting restaurants in all price categories, from the finest silver service to tasty fast foods. Our shopping centres also offer an amazing array of foodstuffs, including many specialty products developed for the Australian market. It is difficult to appreciate how far we have come since the days of Kraft cheddar cheese, Peck's Paste and brawn, for today's shopper has specialty cheese shops, European charcuteries and patisseries with a staggering range of produce.

The meat pie, tank loaf and fish and chips have mercifully given way to the focaccia, the croissant and the char-grilled octopus. When we entertain we also plan and present excellent menus. Our climate is ideal for alfresco dining: what could be better than crisp Australian dry wine, an entrée of seafood antipasto offering Coffin Bay scallops, king prawns, some prosciutto and melon, taramosalata and Italian fried and baked vegetables? For the main meal, what about a stuffed schnapper or a chicken and papaya salad, followed by a summer pudding and King Island cream with a very cold bottle of Australian sweet wine to follow? Of course, there are endless combinations of this and I'm sure you've got the message that Australia's cuisine is indeed the cuisine of the world, presented in the best part of the world.

Sources of Illustrations

The author is grateful to the many people who offered illustrations for inclusion in this book. Special thanks to those unsung advertisers of Australian products whose work is represented here. Every effort has been made to contact copyright owners, but if we have inadvertently overlooked anyone please contact the author. All illustrations included are from the picture and printed book collection of the Mitchell Library, State Library of New South Wales except for: cover detail, private collection; p. 58 author's collection; p. 64 Max Dupain; p. 119 author's collection.